CW00918290

From Bow Street to the Ritz:
Oscar Wilde's Theatrical Career from 1895 to 1908

From Bow Street to the Ritz:
Oscar Wilde's Theatrical Career from 1895 to 1908

BY

MICHAEL SEENEY

High Wycombe
THE RIVENDALE PRESS
2015

ISBN 978 1 904201 26 7

Copyright © 2015 Rivendale Press

Published by

Rivendale Press
P. O. Box 85
High Wycombe
Bucks HP14 4WZ
England

PRINTED AND BOUND BY CPI GROUP (UK) LTD., CROYDON, CRO 4YY

CONTENTS

ILLUSTRATIONS

Fig. 1 Railway advertisement (from *The Stage Year Book* 1910).

Fig. 2 "On Tour": a Provincial Theatrical Company at a Railway Station, drawn by Frank Reynolds (from *The Graphic*, 30 November 1901).

Fig. 3 David Allen advert (from *The Stage Year Book* 1910).

Fig. 4 Postcard of Beerbohm Tree as Lord Illingworth in the first production of *A Woman of No Importance*.

Fig. 5 *Lady Windermere's Fan*, Her Majesty's Theatre, Aberdeen, 1894.

Fig. 6 Advert for the Theatre Royal, Merthyr Tydfil (from *The Era*, 27 November 1897).

Fig. 7 *Woman of No Importance*, Coronet Theatre, Notting Hill, 1899.

Fig. 8 *The Importance of Being Earnest*, Coronet Theatre, Notting Hill, 1901.

Fig. 9 Fan used by Lilian Braithwaite in *Lady Windermere's Fan*, St. James's Theatre, London, 1904.

Fig. 10 *Lady Windermere's Fan*, St. James's Theatre, London, 1904.

Fig. 11 *Lady Windermere's Fan*, Act III, St. James's Theatre, London, 1904.

Fig. 12 *The Importance of Being Earnest*, Crystal Palace Theatre, London, 1902.

Fig. 13 *The Importance of Being Earnest*, Imperial Theatre, London, 1903.

Fig. 14 "Wright & Jones" advertisement for works by Oscar Wilde, Imperial Theatre programme, 1903.

Fig. 15 Advert for the Marquis of Anglesey's *An Ideal Husband* (from the *Bournemouth Observer and Chronicle*, 27 November 1903).

Fig. 16 *An Ideal Husband*, Coronet Theatre, Notting Hill, 1905.

Fig. 17 *An Ideal Husband*, New Theatre, Cambridge, 1905.

PLATES

Plate 1 *The Importance of Being Earnest* Coronet Theatre, Notting Hill, 1901.

Plate 2 & 3 A pair of posters for *A Woman of No Importance* (probably 1898).

Plate 4 *An Ideal Husband*, New Theatre, Cambridge, 1905.

INTRODUCTION

On 5 April 1895 Oscar Wilde was the most successful playwright in Britain. He had two plays running on the West End stage and his earlier comedies were touring the provinces. *An Ideal Husband* had opened at the Haymarket Theatre on 3 January and *The Importance of Being Earnest* at the St James's on 14 February. Both were doing good business. *An Ideal Husband* was playing at the Lyceum Theatre in New York and *The Importance of Being Earnest* was due to open there at the Empire Theatre on 22 April.[1] In the afternoon of 5 April Wilde was arrested. The following morning the British press reported that

> The two plays by Oscar Wilde – "An Ideal Husband" and "The Importance of Being Earnest" – at present on the London stage, although performed as usual last night, have since been withdrawn from the playbills of the St James's and Haymarket Theatres respectively, and will not be repeated. The idea of reproducing the "Ideal Husband" at the Criterion has also been abandoned.

In New York Wilde's name similarly disappeared from *An Ideal Husband* programmes. In London, by long standing arrangement, *An Ideal Husband* was to close that day. Conscious that the public would assume the closure was connected to Wilde's arrest, the management of the Haymarket Theatre countered with a letter to the editor of *The Morning Post* on 8 April in which they said:

> Sir, - As there appears to be some misconception as to whether we intend to carry out our arrangements entered into some time ago to transfer "An Ideal Husband" at the end of our tenancy of this theatre to another house, we should like to state that we do not feel justified in making large numbers of people suffer by altering our plans, and that we shall therefore adhere to our engagements and play the piece at the Criterion on Saturday, April 13. "An Ideal Husband" is an entirely innocent play, which has been accepted by the public and the Press as an agreeable evening's entertainment, and has already been performed over 100 times.
>
> Yours, &c., Lewis Waller and H H Morell

---

1 The play duly opened with Wilde's name in small print on the programme, but closed after a week.

An Ideal Husband duly transferred on 13 April to the Criterion Theatre, where Wilde's name was restored to the programmes. *The Stage* reported that the play "called together a large audience"; but it ran for only two weeks, finally closing on 27 April. It was followed on 7 May by R.C. Carton's *The Home Secretary*.

The Importance of Being Earnest continued playing at the St James's Theatre until 8 May by which time it had been performed eighty three times. Three days later it was replaced by Henry Arthur Jones's *The Triumph of the Philistines*, which ran for 39 performances.

And that, if the majority of works on Wilde are to be believed, was that for the four comedies until the next century. Robert Tanitch, in his *Oscar Wilde on Stage and Screen*, shows no productions of *The Importance of Being Earnest* and *Lady Windermere's Fan* between their first outings and 1901; no subsequent production of *A Woman of No Importance* until 1903 and none of *An Ideal Husband* until 1914.

The impression given by commentators and biographers is that until 1901 Wilde's comedies disappeared, and even then returned one by one as experiments to see whether the public was ready for them. Joseph Bristow in the recent *The Reception of Oscar Wilde in Europe* says:

> Tree's 1907 production at Her Majesty's Theatre, which received mixed reviews, reveals the enduring public interest in Wilde's society comedies, which had resumed as early as 1901 with performances of *Lady Windermere's Fan* and *The Importance of Being Earnest* at the Coronet Theatre, London.

Montgomery Hyde in his biography *Oscar Wilde* talked of George Alexander buying the copyrights of *Lady Windermere's Fan* and *The Importance of Being Earnest* for a small sum at the time of the bankruptcy because although

> he knew that he could not put them on with any chance of a satisfactory return for some time, he also realised that he had two potentially valuable properties which were bound to appreciate in value if he kept them long enough.

Noreen Doody, again in *The Reception of Oscar Wilde in Europe* says

> Wilde's name is seldom mentioned in the Irish media during the following ten years [1895-1905] and not at all in the Irish Times until 1905, five years following his death... .

> In July 1907 the Gaiety Theatre announced that 'Oscar Wilde's brilliant plays' would be playing for one week at the theatre in matinee and evening performances. *Lady Windermere's Fan* and

> *The Importance of Being Earnest*, which had been performed in Ireland in 1901 by the visiting company of George Alexander at the Theatre Royal Dublin and the Grand Opera House Belfast, were welcomed to the Dublin stage in the week of 2 September 1907

We will see that several places in Ireland continued to advertise and stage Wilde's plays throughout those ten years.

Perhaps the only biographer to have understood the true situation with regard to the plays was Leonard Cresswell Ingleby who, in his 1907 biography of Wilde said of *A Woman of No Importance*:

> As literature alone, the play deserves to live, and will live, as a *pièce de théâtre*. It has met with more success than any play of the first class within the last twenty years. The reason for that is not far to seek – it is essentially human, and the woman's interest – the keynote of the story – appeals to man and woman equally. I have seen rough Lancashire audiences, bucolic boors in small country towns, and dour headed Scotsmen, sit spellbound as the story of the woman's sin and her repentance was unfolded before them.

I hope to show just where and when those audiences may have been so affected by that and Wilde's other comedies.

What is true is that, following the early example of removal from programmes and posters, Wilde's name largely disappeared from the stage for many years. But the plays, as this book shows, continued to be popular throughout the remainder of Wilde's life and beyond.

The title of this book is "From Bow Street to the Ritz", delineating the period between Wilde's arrest and the dinner at the Ritz on 1 December 1908 celebrating Ross's acquisition of Wilde's copyrights and the publication of the *Collected Works*. During this period the four comedies were not only performed all over Britain and Ireland, but in Australia, New Zealand, India, South Africa and China. The story of productions in America must wait for another volume.

I have limited myself to the four comedies – *Lady Windermere's Fan, A Woman of No Importance, An Ideal Husband* and *The Importance of Being Earnest* – because with the exception of a very few private club performances of *Salome*, no other Wilde plays appear to have been performed in Britain during this period. The first production of another work of his was Lou Tellegen's production of Constant Lounsbery's adaptation of *The Picture of Dorian Gray* at the Vaudeville Theatre in London in 1913.

Little work has been published on touring theatre of this period, so the first chapter attempts to provide some background on the structure, economics and administration behind the performance of these plays. The following chapters look at the press reaction to the productions in London in 1895; the touring companies and theatres that made up the British and Irish touring circuit around the turn of the nineteenth century; the touring productions of each of the Wilde comedies and the slow return of those plays to the West End.

This book would not have been possible without the British Library's online database of British newspapers and the similar one provided by the National Library of Australia. There is more work to be done; it is clear that dates for some tours are more complete than for others, and a full study needs to be done of Wilde in America.

1. TOURING AT THE END OF THE 19TH CENTURY

The nineteenth century was a time of profound change in the theatre as well as in most other aspects of British life. In his history of the Actors' Association, Joseph Macleod described the situation in the first half of the century:

> England, Scotland, and to some extent Wales and Ireland also, were covered with small, permanent theatrical units. Some were mobile, with no premises of their own, continually on the move, in more or less fixed and regional circuits of short seasons, or weeks, or two-night stands. Even little towns like Newport Pagnell, Alloa and Huntingdon had premises of some kind, occupied week after week by different companies, with eager audiences to receive them; small theatres, assembly rooms, halls, or, in the humblest case of Helensburgh, the large room of an inn, proudly if misleadingly entitled 'The Theatre', or even 'Theatre Royal'.[1]

Standards were remarkably variable but the better ones grew and began to remain in one place, taking longer leases or occasionally buying premises. Centred on a provincial city and touring the immediate area in the off season, they formed what Macleod called "a kind of aristocracy in local companies". It was from these companies that the stock companies grew. According to Ellen Terry, who had joined one in Bristol in 1861 at the age of fifteen, a stock company was

> a company of actors and actresses brought together by the manager of a provincial theatre to support a leading actor or actress – "a star" – from London.[2]

Henry Arthur Jones, in 1901, remembered

> When I became a provincial playgoer in 1870 the old circuit system had been dead for nearly a generation and the stock company system was already dying. … I was able to watch the transition in the provinces from the stock company located for a season in one town and playing a repertory, to our present system of travelling companies moving from town to town and

---

1 *The Actor's Right to Act*, Joseph Macleod, Lawrence and Wishart, 1982, p. 15.

2 *Ellen Terry's Memoirs*, preface and notes by Edith Craig and Christopher St John, Victor Gollancz 1933, p. 35.

playing only one of the recent London successes.[3]

Most of the tours described in this book are a compromise, in that they move from town to town but take a repertory of plays, mainly (fairly) recent London successes.

Jones may have learned about the stage from stock companies, but he did not flinch from criticising them

> The scenery and furniture were atrociously bad. A shabby orange-coloured chamber nightly challenged every law of architecture, decoration, and archaeology; brazenly pretending to be a mid-Victorian parlour tonight, while last evening it had claimed to be Joseph Surface's library, and the night before it had ambitiously posed as Portia's palace. ... the Forest of Arden might perhaps have passed muster as the ramparts of Elsinore if it had not been unblushingly announced the week before as the "Exterior of a Cottage at Clapham;" at the same time showing a background of wonderful rocky sea ravine such as no Rosalind nor any maiden of South London has ever gazed upon.[4]

The star might stay for a season or, if a really big star, for one night only. It would be up to the star whether to bother to rehearse with the company. "A very unequal and slovenly performance, except in the leading parts, was generally the result," thought Jones, from the pit. But the company was nothing if not versatile. Squire Bancroft, later to become one of the major players in the theatrical world, also joined a stock company in 1861 (in Birmingham). From January to July he played thirty six different parts. In thirty six nights in Cork he played forty parts – three hundred and forty six parts in four years four months.

There had also been a problem with audiences. The theatre in the first half of the century had been largely deserted by the growing middle classes and, as Julie Holledge says in her book on Edwardian actresses, the task of wooing them back

> was taken up by the actor-managers. It was these performers, rather than writers or producers, who dominated Victorian theatre. In order to go into management, actors had to convince a financial backer that their popularity with the theatre-going public was sufficient to warrant leasing a theatre. It was not

---

3 *The Foundations of a National Drama*, Henry Arthur Jones, Chapman and Hall, 1913, p. 222.

4 Ibid., p. 225.

unusual for the lease of a minor theatre to change hands within three years. In contrast, the major theatres were often leased by the same actor-manager for over twenty.[5]

By 1895 a certain amount of respectability had been conferred on the theatre as a profession, culminating in that year with the granting of a knighthood to Henry Irving, with the same honour being conferred in the following years on Beerbohm Tree, George Alexander, and other actor-managers. The children of the middle class were beginning to contemplate a career in the theatre, and the late Victorian and Edwardian period saw a great many younger sons and daughters of Society parents become actors.

Claire Cochrane has written about "an unselfconscious provincialism", in which an "unexamined prejudice has driven much British theatre history to skew the record towards the assumption that everything important in British theatre happened in London".[6] It is certainly true that remarkably little has been written about theatrical touring companies in the late Victorian and early Edwardian period. Their productions were ephemeral; the players were not, for the most part, stars; management, both of companies and theatres, was far from transparent; and many of the theatres in which they played are no more. Probably the best known touring company was the fictitious one run by Vincent Crummles in *Nicholas Nickleby*; certainly by the period dealt with here, he and his "infant phenomenon" were not typical of the troupes doing the rounds of provincial theatres.

Touring companies were what kept the theatre alive outside London. A tradition had grown up of locally produced pantomimes of increasing complexity and spectacle at many of the larger provincial theatres. But while they were very effective money makers and, usually starting on Boxing Day (26 December) might run until Easter, there was still three quarters of the year to fill.

The West End was held up as the crucible in which theatrical advances were forged, and while there were short term financial gains to be made, the longer term was not necessarily as rosy. Wilde's bankruptcy statement suggests that he earned something over £1,600 for the West End run of *An Ideal Husband*; a substantial amount in a relatively short time.[7] On

---

5 *Innocent Flowers*, Julie Holledge, Virago, 1981 p. 7.

6 *Twentieth Century British Theatre*, Claire Cochrane, Cambridge University Press, 2011, p. 2.

7 *Oscar Wilde's Profession: writing and the culture industry in the late nineteenth*

the other hand, as Tracy C Davis has pointed out, Henry Irving mounted lavish and much admired productions for twenty years at the Lyceum and over that period made a net loss of around £20,000. It was his provincial tours which turned the financial tide, giving an overall positive balance of £10,000, representing a profit of only £500 a year.[8]

Henry Arthur Jones, whose plays toured extensively, took a rather jaundiced view of the touring theatre

> The large towns, eight or ten in number, are visited nearly every year by some of the leading London managers – Irving, Tree, Alexander, Hare, the Kendals, the Cyril Maudes, and others. These leading managers take their London productions and their London performers – at any rate in the leading parts. … These visits of the leading actors are almost always crowded, and bring a very substantial profit to both London and local manager. And these few weeks, at most some six or eight in the autumn, are almost the only profitable ones in the whole year for our leading country managers – apart from pantomime and musical comedy. There is perhaps a chance successful week or so of a London success, a popular melodrama, or an extraordinary farce like *Charley's Aunt*.[9]

Jones was making a case for a national drama, so one suspects hyperbole here. The newspaper reports of the attendances at the plays considered in this book paint a different picture.

William Archer devised the "Law of the Hundred Thousand", whereby the mark of a play's success was a run of at least one hundred performances in a theatre seating a thousand. In the days before mass tourism changed the nature of West End audiences, Archer acknowledged that this was never going to be realistic for serious drama, and thus the movement for a subsidised theatre grew.

We know little about the costs of running provincial theatres in this period, but a series of articles in the *St James's Gazette* in early 1885 by someone calling himself "An Old Lessee" give some very detailed insights

---

century, Josephine M Guy and Ian Small, Oxford University Press 2000, p. 125.

8 *The Economics of the British Stage 1800-1914*, Tracy C Davis, Cambridge University Press, 2000.

9 Jones p. 227.

into the economics of West-End theatres.[10]

The rent was the largest predictable outgoing for any theatre, and a number of factors needed to be taken into account in setting a rent – capacity, location and reputation among them. There might also be a complex of sub-lessees between the freeholder and the "working" lessee – the person responsible for staging productions. A reasonable rent in the West-End at that time for a theatre in a good position was about £3000 a year, plus £300 for rates and taxes. Gas – electricity would come in over the next few years – was about £10 a week for plays, more for musical performances or burlesque. As the Old Lessee says:

> We thus come to something very like £80 a week before the manager can stand upon the stage with his hands in his pockets and begin to consider what he will produce.

Leaving aside the costs of performers, the theatre had to pay for "carpenters, property men, gas men, scene shifters and limelight men", although these were usually employed by a master carpenter, or similar depending on the trade, thus freeing the lessee from a lot of the day to day running of the theatre.

The Old Lessee considered the position of business manager to be essential as "no man is harder worked". In the West-End he – always a man - received between £6 and £15 a week, for which he looked after receipts, payments including salaries, and made

> the contracts for advertising and printing, and exercises a general supervision over the check-takers and attendants. He has absolute discretion as to the free list, and must know thoroughly whom to admit without question and when to distribute the gratuitous orders. He has to invent excuses with which to pacify everybody, from the Lord Chamberlain and his officials and the dignitaries of the press down to a troublesome creditor, or it may even be the officer of the Sheriff of Middlesex. His personal attendance at the theatre will occupy him almost incessantly.

Sometimes the question of who to admit went beyond the business manager. W H Leverton, who was at the Haymarket Theatre for many years recalled that, in 1893

> The most difficult first night allotment at which I ever assisted

---

10 *St James's Gazette*, 10 January to 13 February 1885, discussed in "Theatrical Business in the 1880s" by Michael R Booth, *Theatre Notebook*, Vol XLI, No 2, 1987.

was that of Oscar Wilde's play, "A Woman of No Importance."

Wilde came up to Tree's office with a request for something like forty stalls in the best positions – of course to be paid for by him (Wilde). Tree was dubious as to who was going to occupy these seats, and asked Wilde for the names. Oscar was very indignant, and flatly refused to give any names.

"Do you think, my dear Tree, that I'm going to submit the names of my friends for your approval?"

Tree replied that he would certainly have to do so before he could have the seats, saying (which was not his real reason) that some of the people on Wilde's list might have had seats already marked off to them. Wilde refused to give in, and there was a deadlock. Finally, after a hot argument:

"Very well then, Mr Leverton," said Tree, "Mr Wilde doesn't have any seats at all."

Eventually, however, a better temper prevailed on both sides, and the matter was amicably compromised.[11]

There was a great appetite for recent London successes as well as favourite old potboilers. When Wilde started writing West End plays, touring was a relatively new way of satisfying that appetite. Jean Chothia says that in 1879, only thirteen years before the premiere of *Lady Windermere's Fan*, there were only twelve touring companies, but by 1901 "some 205 provincial towns and cities had theatres".[12] Towards the end of 1900 *The Stage* listed 281 companies touring the British Isles (still including Ireland at that time).

A number of factors fed this growth: increasing population, and with it increasing urbanisation; a rapid expansion of the number of theatres and other performance spaces; the developing fashion for seaside holidays; and, most importantly for touring companies, the much improved speed and availability of transport – in particular the railway network. The nature of theatres themselves also contributed, with the slow disappearance of the pit and the introduction of electricity from the 1880s, allowing new lighting effects and a more comfortable auditorium. Lena Ashwell, speaking at a meeting of the New Vagabonds' Club in 1903, said that better lighting in theatres had meant a much closer relationship between stage and audience

11 *Through the Box Office Window*, W H Leverton, Werner Laurie, 1932, p. 67.

12 *English Drama of the Early Modern Period 1890-1940*, Jean Chothia, Longman, 1996, p. 23.

and had made it possible to put on plays which were both more delicate and more real.[13]

Provincial theatres were classified as First Class, Second Class, Third Class or Fit Up, and their status would decide the nature of the touring companies that played there. Beerbohm Tree's tours for example would only play First Class theatres. Where appropriate, Appendix 1 notes the class of the theatres where Wilde's plays were performed.

Between 1895 and 1910 a great many theatres were built or rebuilt and they reflected both urban pride and the increased interest in the drama. Among the First and Second class theatres it was normal to have a seating capacity of between 1,000 and 1,500, and the Grand in Boscombe, which was built as part of a larger complex aimed at the seaside visitor, had a capacity of 2,000.

Fit-ups were different. Ina Rozant, in her lightly fictionalised account of an actress's life on tour, *An Actress's Pilgrimage* says of her first tour

> Only towards the end of the rehearsals, did it dawn upon my amateur brain that the tour was a "Fit-up." The word will be a familiar one to every professional, but for the benefit of the ordinary reader, I may explain that it is what is known as a "small theatre tour." This means that we scarcely ever visited a large town where there was a real theatre, but played in small towns – sometimes little more than villages – where there happened to be a good-sized hall, Assembly Rooms, a Mechanics' Institute with a big room attached, a Corn Exchange, or even a disused and enclosed market building.[14]

Ben Iden Payne, who, in 1902 would appear in a touring production of *The Importance of Being Earnest* before going on to a distinguished theatrical career on both sides of the Atlantic, was introduced to the theatre at the Theatre Royal in Manchester. In his autobiography he left a description of that theatre in 1898.

> [T]he ground floor of English provincial theatres was divided into two parts. In the front were five or six rows of "orchestra stalls," with separate seats comfortably upholstered. At the back of the stalls was a low barrier, behind which was the "pit," where the rest of the audience sat crowded together on benches. The

---

13 *Lena Ashwell: Actress, Patriot, Pioneer*, Margaret Leask, University of Hertfordshire Press, 2012, p. 25.

14 *An Actress's Pilgrimage*, Ina Rozant, T Sealey Clark, 1906, p. 2.

pit was not booked beforehand, so for a popular attraction people assembled hours before the ticket offices were opened. Promptness was rewarded – but at a price. There were three pit doors: the "extra-early doors," which opened fully an hour before the play began; the "early doors," where people were admitted half an hour later; and finally the "ordinary doors," which opened to fill the remaining seats during the last fifteen minutes before curtain time. The price of admission at the Theatre Royal descended from three shillings and sixpence for the extra-early to a shilling for the ordinary doors.[15]

In 1898, Sydney Race's journal records his visit to the Theatre Royal in Nottingham to see *The Sign of the Cross* on a Saturday night. He intended to go to the gallery but was late setting out and arrived half an hour after he intended:

> The doors had not been opened more than five minutes when I got to the Quadrant, and there were two long lines of people stretching right round to the Guardian offices in Sherwood Street! To go into the pit under such conditions was absurd, so with a few blushes I joined the 'queue' – when it had greatly diminished – to the gallery door, thinking that at any rate I should get a comfortable seat. But when I got inside – at about 6.20 – I found every seat taken, and a good number of people standing up behind. There was over an hour to wait for the curtain to rise and with the prospect of seeing only part of the stage at the finish, but there was no help for it, so I held on. ....
> The heat was stifling, the light too bad to read, and nothing more exciting than the frantic rush of an attendant to an individual who was smoking to pass the time along. There was not a scrap of the theatre to be seen beyond the stage, and to see that one was always dodging between people's heads, and there was the pleasant prospect before me of a fearful struggle should a panic start, a not unlikely event in such an overcrowded building.[16]

Reminiscing from the 1920s, Shaw Desmond recalled the excitement of queuing for the Boxing Day pantomime at Drury Lane:

> The show begins at 7.30, doesn't it? and it is now only one of the afternoon. But even if we get killed when the great doors

---

15 *A Life in a Wooden O*, Ben Iden Payne, Yale University Press, 1977, p. 5-6.

16 *The Journals of Sydney Race 1892-1900: a provincial view of popular entertainment*, edited by Ann Featherstone, The Society for Theatre Research 2007, p. 122.

open we are going to get into that pit in order to enter the gates of heaven, with Arthur Collins as Saint Peter, and, as I think, having to pay an extra "tanner" or sixpence for the privilege, for "The Lane" pit was 3s.[17]

At the Coronet Theatre in Notting Hill in 1899 for a performance of *A Woman of No Importance*, the structure of admission prices was complex: cheapest of all was the gallery at 6d; the pit was 1s, pit stalls 2s, the balcony 2s or 2/6, the dress circle 3s or 4s, orchestra stalls 5s and private boxes ranged from 10/6 to 2 guineas.

At the Theatre Royal, Haymarket patrons booking for the front row of the first circle were warned, "Bonnets not allowed", although they were explicitly allowed in other rows of the first circle.

In addition, opera glasses could be hired for 1s per pair and programmes could be purchased. Both of these extras could be purchased from "attendants". It had been common during the nineteenth century to let "front-of-house" to a contractor who would have exclusive rights to sell refreshments and to that end would fit out and stock the bars and provide catering staff. If, as was common, the contractor also had the right to charge cloakroom fees and sell programmes, the contract would, according to Old Lessee, be worth £35 a week to the theatre manager – a steady and predictable income. Towards the end of the century programmes began proudly to say "no fees of any kind", indicating that these practices had ended. When, in 1907, Lena Ashwell took over the Great Queen Street Theatre in London and refurbished it (in the process renaming it the Kingsway Theatre) she made sure she oversaw all refreshments, including afternoon teas served at matinees. By the late 1880s the Theatre Royal, Haymarket included in its programmes the instructions

> NO FEES. The Management particularly requests the Public
> to make no remuneration whatever to Servants.

Otherwise, charging structures seem not to have changed a great deal during the period: at the end of 1903 the Royal County Theatre in Bedford was advertising that doors would open at 7:30 but "early doors open at 7 to all parts, 6d extra." One new feature in this advertisement was "children under 12 half-price to all parts, except Gallery".

In 1899 Ben Iden Payne joined his first touring company and described the excitement of his first day:

---

17 *London Nights in the Gay Nineties*, Shaw Desmond, Robert M McBride, 1928, p. 170.

[O]n Sunday morning an early train took me to Crewe Station in plenty of time to meet the company. Crewe, though a small town, is a busy junction on the London and Northwestern Railway. At that time touring was in its heyday. All day long on every Sunday there were frequent arrivals and departures of "theatrical specials," trains made up exclusively of touring companies, each of which was provided with its separate coach and a baggage van attached thereto. On arrival at Crewe the trains were split up. There was much shunting of coaches into new arrangements in preparation for departures in different directions. Consequently, actors could depend upon a long wait in Crewe, and the platforms were centers of excitement as the specials pulled into the station. Actresses rushed frantically from one platform to another to find out what companies were on the newly arrived trains. This was followed by a search for acquaintances and screams of joy when they were found. There were eager inquiries about how much time there would be for chatter and gossip. The men took it more calmly. They generally retired with their friends to the refreshment room to discuss matters over a glass of beer, for as bona fide travellers they could purchase alcoholic beverages during legally restricted hours.[18]

Printed sheets showing the name of the relevant company were pasted on the coach windows and flat metal boxes filled with hot water could sometimes be procured to warm passengers' feet while travelling in winter.

Cicely Hamilton claimed that Derby, rather than Crewe, was the centre of the theatrical universe for train travellers and described the etiquette that existed

> about the allotment of carriages, as about the allotment of dressing-rooms; you were paired off according to your rank and station in the company. In melodrama, when I played the 'heavy,' as I usually did, the leading lady and I shared a carriage as a matter of course.[19]

The extent to which actors used the railways led to a prolonged campaign for lower fares. In 1897 The Music Hall Artistes' Railway Association was formed; members could get a 25 per cent discount off the ordinary fare on railways and steam-boat journeys as well as insurance against injury and loss or damage to luggage when travelling in parties of five or more. Membership was 5s a year, and by 1907 there were over 7,000 members.

---

18 Payne, p. 14.

19 *Life Errant*, Cicely Hamilton, J M Dent 1935, p. 38.

GREAT CENTRAL RAILWAY.

Theatrical Companies & Variety Artists.

SUNDAY EXPRESSES.

The QUICKEST and MOST COMFORTABLE ROUTE

TO AND FROM THE NORTH.

TO AND FROM SOUTH WALES AND THE WEST OF ENGLAND

(Via BANBURY).

TO AND FROM THE EASTERN COUNTIES

(Via LINCOLN and G.E.R., or Via RETFORD and G.N.R.).

DIRECT ROUTE TO THE CONTINENT

(Via GRIMSBY).

Regular Sailings

TO AND FROM HAMBURG, ROTTERDAM, AND ANTWERP.

Reduced Fares for Theatrical Companies and Members of the M.H.A.R.A.

APPLY BY THE COMPANY'S STEAMSHIPS.

In addition to the Ordinary Express Service, numerous **Special Trains** are run for the **Convenience of Theatrical Companies and Variety Artists,** and Managers who have not already done so are invited to send particulars of their Tours to **Mr. W. BARTON, Theatrical Traffic Agent, Marylebone Station, N.W.** (Telephone **Paddington 600**). The Great Central Railway have specially constructed Trucks to accommodate scenery of long length.

Fig. 1 Railway advertisement (from *The Stage Year Book* 1910).

Julia Neilson, who created the role of Lady Chiltern in *An Ideal Husband* toured extensively but hardly mentions it in her autobiography:

> On tour [1896] Alexander used to take his company round 'in the grand manner' – a special train and first-class coaches: an unknown luxury in those days for the touring actor, who, on those interminable Sunday journeys, which usually started in the pale dawn and ended a long time after dewy eve – since all trains seemed to be given precedence of 'the theatricals' – was generally worn out by the time he reached his destination. I may add that this praiseworthy example of Alexander's was emulated by Fred and myself, when we began to take our own company on tour; we started off very grandly – special train, first-class coaches and a diner for the longer journeys; no 'fish and actors in the sidings' for us! But when the war of 1914 broke out and expenses became ruinous, we had to economize. We still occasionally had our specials and our diners, but the coaches were third-class, though the comfort of railway accommodation had so increased by then that I don't think any of us found it a hardship. Our rule remained – four to a carriage, which meant that everyone had a corner, and Fred and I each had a carriage to ourselves, where we could rest or learn parts, if we wanted. Fred, however, was always away, down the train, with some of the 'boys and girls', playing his beloved poker; and later on he and I did most of the journeys in our Rolls – christened by the company 'the Royal Car'. The 'boys and girls' continued to be well looked after by our manager, Garrett, and I think the comfort of our transport system was envied by a good many of the companies whom we encountered on Sundays 'on the road'.[20]

The Marquis of Anglesey took the "Royal Car" style of touring to new levels in 1903, as will be seen in a later chapter.

F Kinsey Peile, who played the manservant Lane in the first production of *The Importance of Being Earnest*, wrote about touring in his autobiography and clearly had a more pleasant time than Julia Neilson:

> In the Victorian days, when London or, at any rate, the West End of London, was deserted in the month of August, all the houses closed and nothing to be seen but a solitary policeman and a few stray cats; the theatrical world took its cue from the West End and shut up shop too. Most of the theatres were closed for repairs, cleaning, and decoration, preparatory to the autumn

---

20 *Time for Remembrance*, Julia Neilson, Hurst and Blackett, 1940, p. 151.

Fig. 2 "On Tour": a Provincial Theatrical Company at a Railway Station, drawn by Frank Reynolds (from *The Graphic*, 30 November 1901).

productions; actors and actresses took a few days' well-deserved holiday before commencing work for the tours, which generally began on or about Bank Holiday. The actor-managers of the leading theatres, with their entire London companies, would set out for a round of the large provincial towns, taking with them their latest London success or a small repertoire of plays.[21]

Peile later became a successful playwright, having never moved up the acting hierarchy, but clearly enjoyed his touring days:

> George Alexander used to organise a provincial tour of this description, and very delightful it was. He travelled *en prince*; had his own special train, composed of saloon or first-class carriages, with third-class carriages for the staff, and vans for the scenery. When the train arrived at some large provincial town, it was often met by the mayor and corporation, with red baize spread and bouquets presented. The best hotels were always ready to make special terms for any artistes who elected to go to them, and theatrical lodgings, very comfortable and cheap, abounded. Those were the good old days, a happy dream compared to the nightmare which touring has now become, with its uncomfortable train journeys in third-class carriages and its exorbitant prices.[22]

Peile travelled with the bigger touring companies; for Ben Iden Payne's first tours the travel was not always as good:

> It was not unusual for us to travel "on the baggage," as the practice was called. The railway would carry us to the next town even though there was no money to pay for our transportation there. But our baggage van was retained in a siding until the fares were paid. On Monday the manager of the theatre would advance the money to free the baggage so that we could open.[23]

The railways made possible another way of taking West-End plays out of London – the flying matinee. George Alexander gave one such performance of *The Importance of Being Earnest* in Brighton in 1895, and Brighton and Crystal Palace seem to have been the usual targets for them; but in 1907 the actress-manager Lena Ashwell determined to push the boundaries. She

---

21 *Candied Peile*, Kinsey Peile, A & C Black, 1931, p. 140. From the punning title of his autobiography we must assume that Peile's name should be pronounced Peel

22 Ibid., p. 140.

23 Payne, p. 22.

had opened her new theatre – the Kingsway – in London with a play by an unknown writer, Anthony Wharton called *Irene Wycherley*, and it made "a lucky hit". She began a series of flying matinees; the first, to Eastbourne, was not unusual, nor was Richmond. Birmingham was a stretch, but the next one was record breaking. She intended to perform in Cardiff at 2:00pm and arrive back in London for the evening performance. They would leave Paddington at 08:45:

> A director of the Great Western Railway will accompany the artists, special printed notices will be circulated ... to the officials all along the line, instructing them to keep the line clear, and four racing motor cars will convey the company from Paddington to the Kingsway along a route which will be specially watched by the police. Every second is precious to make this record breaking performance a complete success. The fourteen artists and five assistants will change dresses and makeup in a specially fitted saloon while travelling at sixty miles an hour. It will be one long, nerve straining, strenuous struggle which only the highest physiques could endure. But it will be done – unless fog makes quick travelling impossible.[24]

This was a success, and the highly organised and publicised feat was repeated the following month with a flying matinee in Coventry.

Payne noted that most actors could only dream of the West End and therefore "anticipated only an indefinitely continuing life on tour".

> Consequently, one of their most closely guarded possessions was a notebook containing an alphabetically arranged list of provincial towns with the names and addresses of landladies to be found there. Sometimes there was an added note about the price paid and the quality of the accommodations. It was a proof of affection for an actor to let another actor see and copy from his book.[25]

Payne seems to have liked his lodgings. Joseph Macleod gives a different view:

> In many cases [landladies] were hostile; in most, suspicious. Because actors make for the immediate neighbourhood of their place of work, the lodgings would generally be near the theatre; and commercial speculators generally built their theatres in neighbourhoods where the ground was cheap. So that the

---

24 Leask, p. 62-63.

25 Payne, p. 16.

landladies too were poor folk, living on a narrow margin and therefore on their sharpness of wit. The sanitation of the rooms they let out, the smells, the bugs, the dirt, the absence of even a hip-bath, made them a byword in an era of wretched lodgings.[26]

Cicely Hamilton, later to become a playwright, remembered the problems of finding theatrical digs

> It was only in the 'smalls,' where theatrical entertainment was irregular, that the problem of 'digs' was acute; in larger towns, where companies arrived and departed each Sunday with clockwork regularity, our needs were catered for by the 'theatrical' landlady – a class distinct from the ordinary letter of lodgings. The theatrical landlady made no bones about late hours, late suppers, or late breakfasts; she cooked her lodgers' dinner at whatever odd hour they asked for it, and made their beds at whatever odd hour they got up.[27]

But for actors in the 'smalls,' where she began her acting career, things were different

> All touring actors are nomads, but the fit-up actor led the life nomadic in extreme; since the 'smalls' he played in could only supply an audience for one or two performances, it was a case of constant moving on and constant finding of lodgings. That hunting for lodgings in the fit-ups was sometimes an exhausting misery; in small seaside towns, for instance, which we were apt to visit in the height of their season, when the place was full and business likely to be good; or in districts where the landladies, for reasons of their own, were shy of 'theatricals,' and preferred not to take them in.[28]

In 1893 the lead actors in touring companies playing to Number One theatres were paid £10 or £15 a week and other actors £2 a week. For Number Two or Three companies the leads received £6 and £7 and others £1 10s. A jobbing actor, touring with a reasonable company would not necessarily be in employment for fifty two weeks of the year, and therefore might expect to earn just under £100 a year. The cost of lodgings ranged from six to ten shillings a week (slightly less than twice that for a couple, which was not unusual). However, the *Sunday Times* claimed in 1893 that

---

26 Macleod, p. 35.

27 Hamilton, p. 36.

28 Hamilton, p. 35.

of some eight or ten thousand actors and actresses, not more than half were in employment at any one time.

Cyril Maude, recalling from the 1920s his early days in "a second-rate little fit-up company taken round the smaller towns by Mr Tom Smale and his wife", remembered

> We carried our own proscenium and scenery, and used to play mostly in small town halls. I got twenty-five shillings a week, and, with a pound a week from my mother, managed to exist. I remember three of us living together, I think it was at Greenwich, one week, and our bill at the end of it worked out at sixteen shillings each – and we had fed well too![29]

But Maude, even in those early days, had some advantages

> Occasionally in those days I would get myself a Sunday evening off in town, and find myself dining at a rich uncle's, where the footmen were in plush breeches, silk stockings, and powdered hair. I used to think how much better fed the footmen were than I was, and glance down anxiously at the frayed silk of my dress coat.[30]

Cicely Hamilton started working in provincial theatre in the early nineties and, looking back from 1935 observes another aspect of touring life

> I have sometimes heard it remarked, with approval, that the stage is the one calling which observes the principle of equal pay for equal work, and makes no difference in its treatment of women and of men. The idea, unfortunately, is not in accordance with the facts; stars – players who are box-office attractions – are in a class apart, and their salaries are estimated not by considerations of sex, but by their power of drawing the public. With the lesser fry of the provinces, however, whose names have no drawing power, the rule obtains that the average woman is paid less than the average man. That was the ordinary practice in my time, and though the difference may have levelled up since then, I am sure that it still exists .... [I]n my time – and possibly today – the touring actress, on her lesser wage, often had heavier expenses than the touring actor; in companies which ran costume plays, clothes would be provided for the men of the cast, the women often had to find their own – and, if their

---

29 *Behind the Scenes with Cyril Maude*, Cyril Maude, John Murray 1927 p. 58.

30 Ibid., p. 59.

dresses were not considered suitable, the management looked at them askance. In modern plays matters were more equal, as both men and women were expected to find their own theatre clothes, except in the case of London successes touring with the wardrobe of the original production.[31]

A particular highlight for Peile, and one which other companies experienced, was the summons to perform for royalty. While Alexander's company was rehearsing at Glasgow (in 1895 or later because the repertoire included Henry Arthur Jones's play, *The Triumph of the Philistines*, the play which had followed *The Importance of Being Earnest* at the St James's Theatre) the call came for a special performance of *Liberty Hall* at Balmoral.

> Arrangements began at once, as special scenery had to be made and painted to suit the small stage at Balmoral and a special installation of gas had to be carried with us to light the stage.[32]

Everything went well, although there was "a strange air of unreality to the performance" because nobody applauded until the Queen applauded and nobody laughed until the Queen laughed. Fortunately she did both frequently. Afterwards:

> George Alexander received a beautiful silver and blue enamel cigar-box as a memento of this occasion; Mrs Alexander, a crystal parasol handle set with diamonds. We most of us got handsome pins; mine was of red enamel set with diamonds.[33]

Peile doesn't mention whether they were paid in the normal way for this extra performance.

If a company was performing a week's run at a new theatre it would begin on a Monday and travel was therefore on a Sunday. The perils of moving the troupe by train were recorded by *The Star* in October 1900, by which time Peile's "good old days" were over:

THEATRICAL TRAIN IN A COLLISION

> On Sunday night the 8.53 train from Gunnersbury, on the Hounslow loop line, ran into the up train from Reading, to which were attached several carriages conveying Messrs Morrell and Mouillot's "Geisha" Company travelling from Bristol to Kingston.
>
> The Central News Twickenham correspondent says the trucks

---

31 Hamilton, p. 43.

32 Peile, p. 142.

33 Peile, p. 148.

containing the scenery were in front, which saved the actors and actresses from the worst effects of the smash. One member of the company, however, was injured, and now lies in Twickenham Hospital. Others were cut and shaken. The guard's van of the Hounslow train was wrecked, but the guard, as well as the driver and firemen, escaped with slight injury. The lines were cleared yesterday morning.

In London other forms of transport were important; Lena Ashwell advertised her newly refurbished Kingsway Theatre as being close to "LCC trams and a fine service of horse and motor buses" and with another line of buses running from Victoria to Kings Cross passing the door.

For the most part, those who have recorded their memories of touring were travelling with, or at least under the protection of, West End managers. Iden Ben Payne, travelling with Mademoiselle Gratienne's small troupe knew a different life, in a company living beyond its means and playing in theatres, some of which "were structures as decrepit as the companies they were able to engage." He explained the company's ability to keep going:

> in spite of the multitude of companies on tour, theatres in the small towns were often hard put to keep open. Even up to Thursday, when *The Stage* was issued, a small-town theatre was sometimes compelled to insert a desperate advertisement offering to book a company for the following Monday! Similarly, the Gratienne company might have reached that day still unbooked. Then there was a hasty exchange of telegrams.[34]

The "necessary posters" were then sent for urgent delivery. Sometimes a small theatre would simply advertise for a whole company – "must dress well" – and stock scenery would be provided by the theatre for whatever play the company knew how to perform.

Payne moved upmarket at the end of a year to join the Benson company. Benson, as Bernard Shaw said had found "that it is better to reign in the provinces than to serve "backer" for fifteen years or so for an uneasy position as a London manager". It wasn't for financial stability that Benson kept to the provinces; he lacked financial skill and "lived on the nerve ends of managerial solvency".[35] Even he found a need, in 1901, to take his

---

34 Payne, p. 23.

35 'Benson's Shakespeare' by Ralph Berry in *British Theatre in the 1890s: essays on drama and the stage*, edited by Richard Foulkes, Cambridge University Press, 1992, p. 184.

Shakespeare to the West End, but the death of Victoria meant audiences stayed away and, despite selling his furniture and pictures to support the company, he returned to the provinces. However, when Benson came to London, Payne suffered as many touring actors did: the small parts he had been playing around the country were taken by more experienced actors. His next move would appear to be going down market again, joining a touring company which specialised in "fit-up" productions. These were normally performed in non-theatrical spaces – corn exchanges, town halls, and the like – in small towns and almost always for one night only, two nights at most. Everything was carried around, including a proscenium, lights, scenery and often a piano. Although no detailed records seem to exist, it would appear that this more leisurely form of touring provided a much better living than the lower end of the touring theatre companies that had provided Payne with his introduction to acting.

While a fit-up company might carry its own piano, in most cases music and musicians had to be arranged at each theatre. *The Musical Times* published an article in 1893 which claimed that "in the average theatre the orchestra holds a very inferior position". At the turn of the century a West End theatre might have an orchestra of between thirty and forty musicians, but elsewhere the norm was closer to that described by Jerome K Jerome in the 1880s where a provincial orchestra "in full force" consisted of "two fiddles, a bass-viol, cornet, and drum". Orchestras were expected to perform for around two hundred nights a year plus matinees, which was incompatible with any other work; they were hired and fired by the musical director (conductor) who was sometimes also responsible for paying them – a practice which led to a deal of mistrust between players and conductors. The players were on low wages and were not paid for rehearsals; if the orchestra could be seen by the audience they were expected to wear evening dress which they had to pay for themselves; and they were allowed to send deputies at any time. Low standards led managements to substitute amateur players and thus contributed to the spiral of decline in theatrical music.

In 1893 both the Orchestral Association and the Amalgamated Musicians' Union were formed but disputes continued. In 1897 the Wigan and District Trades and Labour Council issued a handbill warning "all Trades Unionists" to keep away from the Wigan Theatre Royal "until the dispute between the Old Band and the Management is settled".[36]

---

36 Material in these two paragraphs comes from 'Such a Humble Branch of our Art': The Victorian Theatre Orchestra, David Haldane Lawrence in

A problem which male actors never had to face (one assumes) was described by Cicely Hamilton. She wrote about it in 1935; it was not a problem that would have been openly discussed at the time

> Twice in the course of my life on tour I was thrown out of work to make room for a manager's mistress; no fault was found with the playing of my part, but it was wanted for other than professional reasons, and therefore I had to go.[37]

The emphasis in memoirs on travelling on a Sunday highlights a basic fact of theatre-going in this period, and for many years after. There were no performances on a Sunday. Henry Arthur Jones delivered a lecture entitled "The Licensing Chaos in Theatres and Music Halls" to the National Sunday League in 1910. Beerbohm Tree was in the chair. This was delivered in the light of the successful campaign to have museums and art galleries open on Sundays. Jones was not arguing for plays to be performed on Sundays, but for "common-sense and fair play" to be applied to "the regulation of the people's amusements on their week-day evenings". His argument began

> Inasmuch as theatres and music halls are places where intoxicating liquors are sold; inasmuch also as they are places where large crowds assemble, and there is danger of fire and crushing; inasmuch also as they are places where possibly indecent exhibitions may be held – for all these three reasons it is necessary that there should be a licence to regulate them, so that the Manager may be held responsible for anything taking place there which is indecent, or dangerous, or harmful to the general body of their frequenters. …. But surely this licence should be framed with the idea, and in the intention of not stopping or thwarting any amusement that is not dangerous or harmful or indecent.[38]

He quoted *The Stage Year Book*'s list of "thirteen different ways of licensing Theatres and Music Halls in the United Kingdom", and pointed out the resulting anomalies: a play had to be speedily written to allow a visiting band to play in a venue limited by licence to theatrical presentations; in Holloway the theatre could only produce stage plays (and smoking was banned) but a mile or so away at the Crouch End Theatre "you may smoke and see any kind of entertainment, play or varieties".

Theatre Notebook, Vol. 61, No 1, 2007.

37 Hamilton, p. 47.

38 Jones, p. 270.

Now you know that it is quite illegal for music halls to produce any stage play of any length; but under the illegal agreement between theatre managers and music-hall proprietors – which was condoned by our Chairman – (I am grieved to point him out as a law-breaker) under this illegal agreement Oscar Wilde's "Florentine Tragedy" and Shakespearean scenes are performed at music halls. But theatres may not introduce songs or dances unless they are part of the play.[39]

The solution he proposed to this problem was unexpected

The Theatre Royal, Dublin, is licensed by the Lord Lieutenant of Ireland, and is allowed to present to the public whatever entertainment the manager may find advisable and profitable.

This common-sense arrangement has allowed him to give a dramatic season of high-class plays at a time of the year when his patrons want them. It has allowed him to give a variety entertainment when his patrons ask for a variety entertainment; it has allowed him to give a hippodrome entertainment in the summer, when that form of entertainment is most suitable to the weather and to the tastes of his patrons. The result of this common-sense arrangement has been that the drama has prospered in Dublin, the theatre has paid, and the manager has secured a handsome dividend for the shareholders.

The increasing involvement of local authorities and the influence of watch committees had raised important questions of censorship; Jones admits in this speech that censorship is a problem but confines himself to what he sees as an easy way to simplify the licensing process.

Elsewhere, in trying to encourage better quality theatre in the provinces Jones said

We must not at present expect any aid from municipalities as a body, but perhaps some day it may dawn even upon town councillors that to encourage this most human, civilizing, and in the highest sense educational art, should be as much the business and the ambition of an elected citizen as to lay down drains and build gasworks. Meantime, perhaps, provincial mayors may be entreated to give what encouragement they can to the art of the drama as separate from popular amusement.[40]

Once a company had booked a theatre, knew which play or plays it was

---

39 Jones, p. 274.

40 Jones, p. 240.

to perform and had the cast, scenery, props and music assembled, there was the matter of advertising. For small companies the one or two column inch classified advertisements in the local press were enough, with posters immediately outside the theatre. There were, however, other, more expensive methods. An article in *The Theatre* in 1890 claimed that "there are numerous instances where a play, formerly a failure, has been turned into a success by adroit advertising," and quoted a poem

> Go forth in haste
> With bills and paste,
> Proclaim to all creation
> That men are wise
> Who advertise
> In this our generation.[41]

The article noted three main methods of attracting attention – "journalistic, pictorial, and hand-bill advertisements, and the latter are often paraded and distributed in the west-end of London by means of the humble sandwich-man". The sandwich-man was paid 1s 6d a day but had to keep on the move. If he wore one of the "ridiculous caps" which "actor-managers very unkindly oblige these serfs to carry nowadays" they earned an extra three pence a day. The billposting companies who employed the sandwich-men also employed inspecting foremen at rates of between 2s 6d and 3s a day. The profit to the company for each sandwich-man was somewhere between 3d and 6d a day. When it was announced that Wilde would be touring America in 1882, the newspapers suggested that he was going as d'Oyly Carte's sandwich man.

Theatre advertising seems to have reached something of a peak in 1859 when William Smith, the acting manager of the New Adelphi in London instituted an extraordinary advertising campaign. It consisted of five million handbills, one million cards and ten million adhesive labels. These last "were discovered in omnibuses, cabs, steamboats, vans, railway carriages, refreshment rooms, Windsor Castle, the Old Bailey and upon the glassware of London's restaurants and public houses." He also got his sandwich men to carry heart shaped boards (the play was called *The Dead Heart*). The play was an enormous success.[42]

---

41 'Curiosities of Theatrical Advertising' in *The Theatre*, Vol 16, 1 November 1890.

42 *Inventing the Victorians*, Matthew Sweet, Faber and Faber 2001, p. 44.

A further method of advertising might have been mentioned: the free seat. Old Lessee said, "it may pay you in the long run to fill your house with them for a week or even more" because "they create the idea of a house that is uniformly and steadily filled. People are never so anxious to see a piece as when they believe there is some chance of their not being able to get into the theatre".

Advertising could be very local: the *Western Mail* in March 1895 reported

> The necessity for new methods in advertising is taxing the intellect of the nation. A mysterious carriage was drawn through the streets of Cardiff yesterday, and a notice in each window announced that "This carriage is reserved for "A Woman of No Importance"". Needless to say, the carriage is not reserved for the piece itself, nor for the audience, which is expected to be too big even for the capacious Theatre Royal itself.

The big outlay for advertising, however, was for posters. *The Theatre* went on

> A good deal might be said about pictorial advertisements, one of the largest of which was produced for the Adelphi drama, "The Harbour Lights." It measured twenty feet by fourteen, and represented fifty-six double-crown sheets. It was printed in twenty eight parts, and in five colours. One hundred and forty stones were used, one for each colour, twenty eight times. Each stone cost £5, and weighed seven hundredweight. This huge poster cost something like £600 a thousand. Threepence a sheet was the charge from posting the bill, so that each time it was displayed it cost fourteen shillings, and if fifty copies were posted, which is about the number used in a town like Manchester, Birmingham or Glasgow, the outlay was £35. This is the cost of one bill, and only intended to last a week or two, so our readers can conceive the amount of capital required to take a well-billed play on tour. Nearly £20,000 was spent on pictorial advertisements for "The Silver King," and almost as much for "The Lights o'London."

It should be noted that London is not mentioned. The Old Lessee, who has told us so much about running costs, says that posters were useful in the provinces, but not in London, except at railway stations, where people were forced to wait.

The National Archive holds the copyright application for two posters for *The Importance of Being Earnest* for 1899. Only parts of the images

DAVID ALLEN & SONS

Limited

The LARGEST THEATRICAL and GENERAL
POSTER PRINTERS in the WORLD

LONDON, BELFAST, HARROW, MANCHESTER,
GLASGOW, DUBLIN, BIRMINGHAM, ETC.

Pictorials in Stock to suit any Play, &c., that may be
produced, as well as for all that have been produced
for the last twenty years.

WRITE FOR ILLUSTRATED CATALOGUE

Fig. 3 David Allen advert (from *The Stage Year Book* 1910).

are in the archive, but we can tell that both images were from Act 2, the first showing the argument between Jack and Algy over muffins and the second Gwendolen's complaint about sugar in her tea. Both posters are in full colour and are for A B Tapping's Company. The record gives no indication of size other than that each poster consists of six sheets (three high by two wide). Assuming the sheets to be of the same size as those in the article above, using *The Theatre*'s arithmetic would give, for the two posters together, a price of £250 a thousand and three shillings for posting the two bills. Perhaps even more significant for a poster produced in 1899, both posters include the name of Oscar Wilde.

Posters, using the advances in lithography for printing, were big business and one of the most successful companies was that founded by David Allen in Belfast in 1857. He built his theatre business to the point where it was logical to open a London office in 1888.[43] A Manchester office followed in 1893, with agencies in Australia and America to deal with overseas orders. In 1894, when the volume of printing became too great for the Belfast works, a second works opened in Harrow. Even allowing for all this investment, profits by 1896 were over £20,000 a year. Around

43 Information about David Allen comes from *David Allen's: The History of a Family Firm* by W E D Allen, John Murray, 1957.

this time David Allen & Sons entered into a syndicate with Morrell and Mouillot (see chapter 3), which became known as The Dublin Theatres Company, to acquire theatrical interests in Dublin. Allens offered a long-term printing contract worth £2000 as their contribution to the syndicate's capital. This profitable venture allowed the formation of the David Allen Theatres Company, which invested in entertainment concerns (including early cinemas), built the Broadway Theatre in Deptford, South London and, in time acquired the freeholds of the Theatre Royal in Bournemouth and Leamington, and the Grand Theatre in Swansea and Southampton. In addition the company bought out bill posting companies throughout Britain, thus integrating a number of aspects of the business in a way which had not been seen before.

Bill posting around the turn of the century was an oddly tempestuous business. The growth in the powers of local authorities and various efforts to regulate the business of bill posting led to the formation of the United Billposters' Association, in part as a reaction against the actions of the National Vigilance Society and the well-intentioned but ineffectual National Society for Checking the Abuses of Public Advertising, whose proposed legislation giving local authorities control over the size and siting of billboards in reality gave those authorities a role in censorship. There was also a trade newspaper, imaginatively called *The Billposter*.

The twin posters -see plates 2 & 3 - for *A Woman of No Importance* were produced by David Allen, possibly for the 1894 tour, but more probably for the Beatrice Homer tour of 1898. Nothing should be read into the absence of Wilde's name on either poster; it was common practice to omit an author's name from lithographed posters such as these.

Many touring companies were set up simply to tour one play or a group of plays; they had a natural life for a season or two. Others lasted longer, or intended lasting longer. Cicely Hamilton again reminds us of a downside to the touring actor's lot

> One of the tragedies of stage life in its less exalted spheres was the company left on the road – usually by a manager who made himself scarce when he found himself unable to pay salaries. All sudden throwing out of work is tragic, but in the case of the stranded actor there was an added element of misery: he owed money to his landlady for lodging, and perhaps for board; he was in a strange place – usually a small one – which offered him no prospect of work; hence a railway fare, more or less heavy,

was added to his other misfortunes.[44]

The sums involved were not necessarily large – Hamilton herself once prevented a company failing completely after a run of poor audiences by lending the tour manager two pounds to cover the cost of transporting the company to the next town, where business picked up. Clearly there were managers willing to cheat their companies, but we have seen no evidence of it among the mainly actor-managers who toured Wilde's plays during this period. They may not have all been financially successful, but they were touring popular material and understood their audiences.

However, as stock companies were dying out at the start of this period; touring companies were, by the end of it, feeling the effects of the growth of cinema and the beginning of the fixed repertory system in provincial theatres.

---

44 Hamilton, p. 48.

2. EARLY 1895 AND THE IMMEDIATE AFTERMATH OF THE TRIALS

On the evening of Monday, 18 February 1895 – the day on which the Marquess of Queensberry left his message for Oscar Wilde at the Albemarle Club – *A Woman of No Importance* was playing at the Theatre Royal, Hartlepool. The company, under the management of Morell and Mouillot had been touring the play since the previous year, although the cast had changed considerably. In 1895 it was first played in Shrewsbury, then across the country to York, a quick trip south to Tunbridge Wells and then back north to Durham, Lancaster, Stockton, Workington and South Shields. Unusually for a touring company at this time there was no repertory of plays. The norm for a six night engagement was for three plays to be performed for two nights each plus one or two matinees. *A Woman of No Importance* was clearly considered a sufficient draw to be performed for six nights in each town.

The term matinee was still quite new, having made its first appearance in 1880. Before that, afternoon performances – usually beginning at 2pm – were confusingly known as morning performances, and this was still the case in the provinces for many years. In the West End many managers used the matinee as a space to experiment, staging new plays; Beerbohm Tree saw these matinees as a way of keeping his cast fresh during a long run of a play. By the 1890s, however, the "experimental" matinee had largely left the West End, although they persisted in the suburban theatres and some provincial ones.

In January 1895 the company was already making return visits. The *Yorkshire Herald* said on 9 January:

> After the lapse of some nine or ten months since its first production in York, Mr Oscar Wilde's play, "A Woman of No Importance" was again presented at the York Theatre Royal, yesterday evening. In a play possessing so many striking contrasts, a second visit may have the effect of adjusting the standpoint from which the author's work has probably been judged in the first instance. When witnessed for the first time the two opening acts seem perhaps to present an impossible combination of characters, with an equally impossible facility for smart conversation.

Arguing that the first two acts had shortcomings, "clever and ingenious as much of the dialogue undoubtedly is", the author concluded that it "is when the play is comprehended as a whole that one recognises not only the touch of a master hand in the limning of so tragic a picture of human sin and its expiation, but also the subtle instinct of the artist in the force of the contrasts which the play presents."

Wilde had agreed financial details for a provincial tour of *A Woman of No Importance* on 13 October 1892 in replying to Beerbohm Tree's proposed terms. He assigned to Tree "the rights in my play entitled A Woman of No Importance for performance in Great Britain and Ireland, on condition that you produce it at the Haymarket Theatre," and agreed royalties to be paid dependant on the level of weekly gross receipts. For touring productions the agreement was different:

> In the provinces of Great Britain and Ireland, the said play shall be our joint property, but if you elect to play it yourself in the provinces you shall pay me 5% of the gross receipts.[1]

Josephine M Guy and Ian Small have detailed these financial arrangements as they applied to the touring productions of *A Woman of No Importance* in 1893.[2] Rather than pay Wilde a royalty, there was a fairly crude profit-sharing agreement. The touring company would make a deduction from receipts for expenses and declare a profit (or loss) for each performance. The touring company then took fifty per cent of the profit, with Wilde and Tree taking twenty-five per cent each. There is no indication of whether losses would have been shared in the same way. As we have seen in the chapter on touring structures, the book-keeping and financial probity of some touring companies was at best questionable; in the process by which Tree and Alexander leased touring rights there was presumably some criterion applied to assure them of the touring company's financial standing.

In the absence of evidence to the contrary, similar terms are assumed to apply to the *Woman of No Importance* tour in early 1895.

As part of the bankruptcy proceedings, Wilde signed a Deficiency Account on 10 August 1895. In it, presumably on the assumption that his sentence meant the end of his literary career, royalties which might be earned on future productions of publication of the four comedies were noted as "present value nil". There was a proviso included that George Alexander had a lien on royalties from *Lady Windermere's Fan* and *The*

---

1 "Oscar Wilde's Contract for A Woman of No Importance", Joel H Kaplan in *Theatre Notebook* Vol XLVIII, No 1 1994 pp. 46 et seq.

2 *Oscar Wilde's Profession: writing and the culture industry in the late nineteenth century*, Josephine M Guy and Ian Small, Oxford University Press, 2000, p. 117.

Fig. 4 Postcard of Beerbohm Tree as Lord Illingworth in the first production of *A Woman of No Importance*. Private Collection.

Importance of Being Earnest. The Statement of Proofs showed a balance due to Waller and Morell for royalties from *An Ideal Husband* of £41.9s.4d.[3]

During 1894 and 1895 another *Woman of No Importance* had been touring. Miss Lillie Napier (Mrs Tom Maltby, wife of her promoter) was described as rendering "most creditably songs of a serio-comic class; whilst her sensational dramatic scene, "A Woman of No Importance" has been most favourably received". For this latter, "a splendid scene, representing the Tower Bridge, has been prepared". Unfortunately we do not know what part the bridge played in her presentation.

The popularity of the touring plays – no doubt bolstered by news of Wilde's latest successes in the West End – can be judged from the *Western Mail* on 15 March:

> Next Monday Oscar Wilde's masterpiece, "A Woman of No Importance," will pay its return visit to the Theatre Royal. The play is well remembered by Cardiff playgoers, and many have been anxiously awaiting the revisit of this marvellous piece of dramatic literature. It is nearly a year ago since we were delighted with Mr Wilde's greatest work, and playgoers showed their appreciation of the author and the company interpreting him by nightly crowding the theatre. It is more than anticipated that the same will occur this visit, and to avoid inconvenience or disappointment the box plan was opened on Thursday, and it is advisable that those desiring to be present on the opening night should secure their seats early.

On 4 April *The Importance of Being Earnest* received its first performance outside London, at the Theatre Royal, Brighton. This featured the St James's cast and was a "flying matinee", as described in chapter 1.

So, by the time of Wilde's arrest on 5 April, all four of his comedies had been performed beyond the West End. Both *Lady Windermere's Fan* and *A Woman of No Importance* had enjoyed successful tours throughout 1894. It had even been confidently claimed in August 1894 that *A Woman of No Importance* was "being translated into German, Italian and Spanish, with a view to its early production on the Continent."[4]

---

3 "Heading for Disaster: Oscar's Finances, Chapter Five: Bankruptcy", Donald Mead in *The Wildean* No 46, January 2015, p. 92.

4 *A Woman of No Importance* was less popular in Europe than the other comedies; the first German production was in 1903, Italian in 1906 and Spanish in 1917. *The Reception of Oscar Wilde in Europe*, edited by Stefano Evangelista, Continuum, 2010 pp. lxxvii et seq.

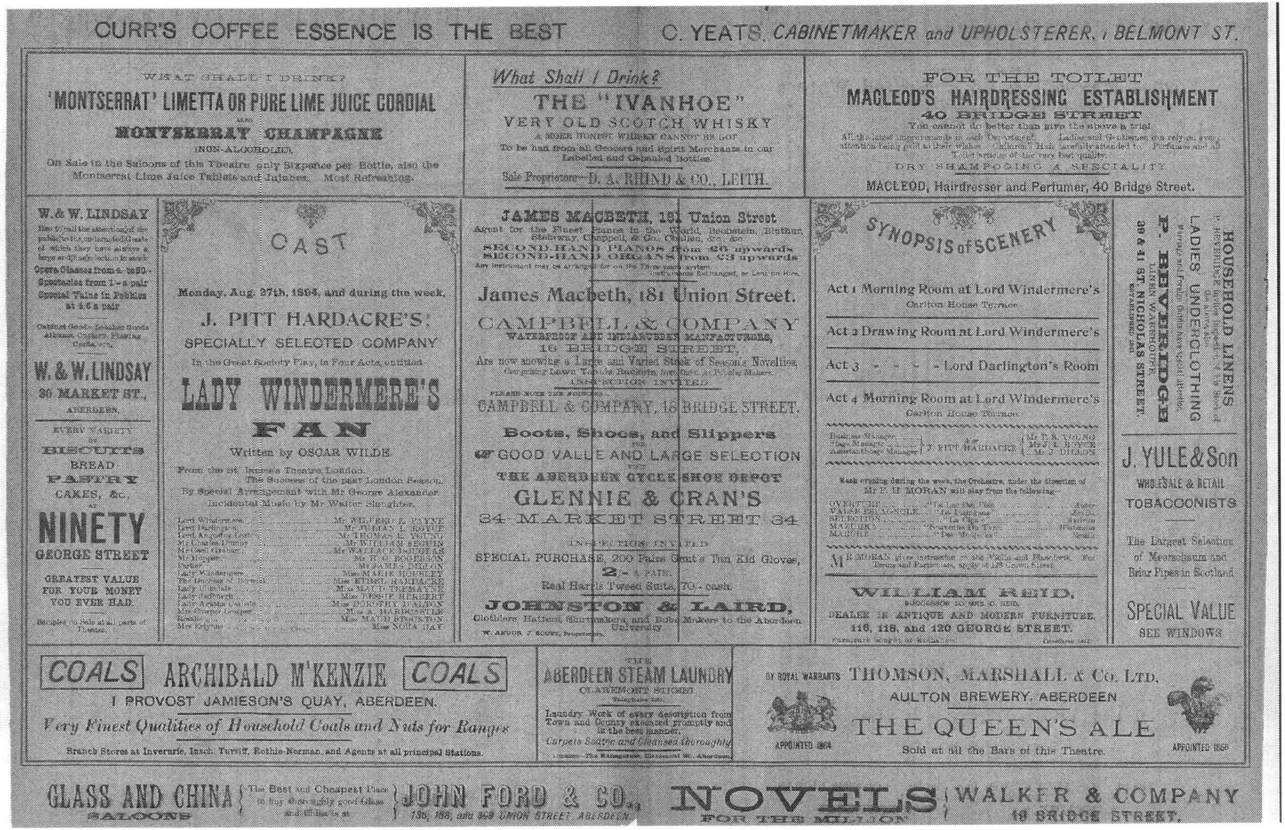
CURR'S COFFEE ESSENCE IS THE BEST
C. YEATS, CABINETMAKER and UPHOLSTERER, 1 BELMONT ST.
WHAT SHALL I DRINK?
'MONTSERRAT' LIMETTA OR PURE LIME JUICE CORDIAL
MONTSERRAT CHAMPAGNE
(NON-ALCOHOLIC).
On Sale in the Saloons of this Theatre only Sixpence per Bottle, also the Montserrat Lime Juice Tablets and Jujubes. Most Refreshing.
What Shall I Drink?
THE "IVANHOE"
VERY OLD SCOTCH WHISKY
To be had from all Grocers and Spirit Merchants in our Labelled and Capsuled Bottles.
Sole Proprietors—D. A. RHIND & CO., LEITH.
FOR THE TOILET
MACLEOD'S HAIRDRESSING ESTABLISHMENT
40 BRIDGE STREET
You cannot do better than give the above a trial.
DRY SHAMPOOING A SPECIALITY.
MACLEOD, Hairdresser and Perfumer, 40 Bridge Street.
W. & W. LINDSAY
Opera Glasses from 4/- to 30/-
W. & W. LINDSAY
30 MARKET ST.,
ABERDEEN.
EVERY VARIETY OF
BISCUITS
BREAD
PASTRY
CAKES, &c.
NINETY
GEORGE STREET
GREATEST VALUE FOR YOUR MONEY YOU EVER HAD.
CAST
Monday, Aug. 27th, 1894, and during the week,
J. PITT HARDACRE'S
SPECIALLY SELECTED COMPANY
In the Great Society Play, in Four Acts, entitled
LADY WINDERMERE'S
FAN
Written by OSCAR WILDE
From the St. James's Theatre, London.
The Success of the past London Season.
By Special Arrangement with Mr George Alexander.
Incidental Music by Mr Walter Slaughter.
JAMES MACBETH, 181 Union Street
SECOND-HAND PIANOS from £6 upwards
SECOND-HAND ORGANS from £3 upwards
James Macbeth, 181 Union Street.
CAMPBELL & COMPANY
16 BRIDGE STREET,
Are now showing a Large and Varied Stock of Season's Novelties,
INSPECTION INVITED
CAMPBELL & COMPANY, 16 BRIDGE STREET.
Boots, Shoes, and Slippers
GOOD VALUE AND LARGE SELECTION
THE ABERDEEN CYCLE SHOE DEPOT
GLENNIE & CRAN'S
34 MARKET STREET 34
INSPECTION INVITED
SPECIAL PURCHASE, 200 Pairs Gent's Tan Kid Gloves,
2/- A PAIR.
Real Harris Tweed Suits, 70/- cash.
JOHNSTON & LAIRD,
Clothiers, Hatters, Shirtmakers, and Robe Makers to the Aberdeen University.
SYNOPSIS of SCENERY
Act 1 Morning Room at Lord Windermere's
Carlton House Terrace
Act 2 Drawing Room at Lord Windermere's
Act 3 - - - - Lord Darlington's Room
Act 4 Morning Room at Lord Windermere's
Carlton House Terrace
J. PITT HARDACRE
Each evening during the week, the Orchestra, under the direction of Mr F. H. MORAN will play from the following—
WILLIAM REID,
DEALER IN ANTIQUE AND MODERN FURNITURE,
116, 118, and 120 GEORGE STREET.
HOUSEHOLD LINENS
LADIES' UNDERCLOTHING
P. BEVERIDGE
LINEN WAREHOUSE
39 & 41 ST. NICHOLAS STREET.
J. YULE & Son
WHOLESALE & RETAIL
TOBACCONISTS
The Largest Selection of Meerschaum and Briar Pipes in Scotland
SPECIAL VALUE
SEE WINDOWS
COALS
ARCHIBALD M'KENZIE
COALS
1 PROVOST JAMIESON'S QUAY, ABERDEEN.
Very Finest Qualities of Household Coals and Nuts for Ranges
Branch Stores at Inverurie, Insch, Turriff, Rothie-Norman, and Agents at all principal Stations.
THE
ABERDEEN STEAM LAUNDRY
CLAREMONT STREET.
Laundry Work of every description from Town and Country executed promptly and in the best manner.
Carpets Beaten and Cleansed thoroughly
BY ROYAL WARRANTS
THOMSON, MARSHALL & Co. LTD.
AULTON BREWERY, ABERDEEN
THE QUEEN'S ALE
Sold at all the Bars of this Theatre.
APPOINTED 1884
APPOINTED 1868
GLASS AND CHINA SALOONS
The Best and Cheapest Place to buy thoroughly good Glass and China is at
JOHN FORD & CO.,
186, 188, and 188 UNION STREET, ABERDEEN.
NOVELS
FOR THE MILLION
WALKER & COMPANY
18 BRIDGE STREET.

Fig. 5 *Lady Windermere's Fan*, Her Majesty's Theatre, Aberdeen, 1894. Private Collection.

On 4 May, by which time Wilde was in Holloway Prison, the *Era* noted that "Miss Lingard celebrated on May Day night at the Theatre Royal, Bath, her 600th performance of Mrs Arbuthnot, with Messrs H H Morell and Frederick Mouillot's "A Woman of No Importance" company."

In September, the *Northern Echo* had said that *Lady Windermere's Fan* provided "one of the most acceptable treats ever enjoyed in Bishop Auckland". If that seems to be damning with faint praise, in Dundee it was claimed in the same month that "*Lady Windermere's Fan* has now taken the place of *A Woman of No Importance* in popular conversation. In this clever piece the characteristics of certain sections of society are well portrayed." In Liverpool, *A Woman of No Importance* "has drawn great audiences." *The Importance of Being Earnest* and *An Ideal Husband* were still in the West End, but the latter had been seen with the West End cast in a morning performance at the Crystal Palace on 28 March, and *Earnest* was seen for a second time – again with the West End cast - at the Theatre Royal, Brighton the day before Wilde's arrest.

The year 1895 therefore promised to be Wilde's theatrical annus mirabilis, but with his arrest on 5 April things appear to change dramatically overnight. But, as we shall see, that may have been true for Wilde but his plays did not suffer the same fate.

London and provincial newspapers on 6 April carried news of Wilde's arrest and differing accounts of the fate of his two current productions. The *North Eastern Daily Gazette* – getting its news from London sources – said "The two plays of Oscar Wilde – "An Ideal Husband" and "The Importance of Being Earnest" – at present running on the London stage, although performed as usual last night, have since been withdrawn from the playbills of the St James's and Haymarket Theatres respectively, and will not be repeated. The idea of reproducing the "Ideal Husband" at the Criterion has also been abandoned". The same newspaper also said confidently (this time getting the plays at the correct theatres) that at "both houses last night his name was omitted from the programme and also from the "posters" outside the theatres". The *Dundee Courier* commented that at neither theatre "was there any hostile demonstration. At the latter theatre [St James's], however, it was noticed that, except in those portions of the building reserved and prepaid, the audience was much smaller than usual". The people of Sheffield, on the other hand, were told that "during the last few days the audiences to witness Wilde's latest dramatic work has been so numerous that the intention of closing the theatre during Holy Week was abandoned."

The St James's had indeed removed Wilde's name, but the Haymarket had not, and the move to the Criterion, which had been planned to allow Beerbohm Tree's return in H C Merivale's adaptation of Sardou's *Fédora*, was confirmed by Lewis Waller and H H Morell in a letter to the Editor of the *Morning Post* on Monday 8 April:

> Sir, - As there appears to be some misconception as to whether we intend to carry out our arrangements entered into some time ago to transfer "An Ideal Husband" at the end of our tenancy of this theatre to another house, we should like to state that we do not feel justified in making large numbers of people suffer by altering out plans, and that we shall therefore adhere to our engagements and play the piece at the Criterion on Saturday, April 13. "An Ideal Husband" is an entirely innocent play, which has been accepted by the public and the Press as an agreeable evening's entertainment, and has already been performed over 100 times. Yours, &c., Lewis Waller and H H Morell, Haymarket Theatre

When the play was performed for the last time at the Haymarket on Saturday 6 April, "a remarkable demonstration was witnessed, the curtain being raised seven times and the audience continuing to applaud until Mr Lewis Waller, one of the managers, came forward and briefly returned thanks on behalf of the company".

At least one newspaper complained at the removal of Wilde's name:

> There is something dismally tragic in its way in the thought of Oscar Wilde in his prison cell whilst two London theatres are crammed with audiences delighted with the clever situations and light persiflage of plays from his pen, in the full tide of their popularity when his career was abruptly cut short. The situation was a little awkward for the managers of St James's Theatre where "The Importance of Being Earnest" is played, and for Messrs Waller and Morell, who had arranged to continue at the Criterion the successful run of "An Ideal Husband." They have attempted to meet it in a manner that is problematically wise, but indubitably mean. They keep on the plays, but erase the name of the dishonoured author.

At the Criterion, where Wilde's name was kept on the programme, the play "called together a large audience". The cast had been retained from the Haymarket, although some were playing different parts:

> Miss Featherston now takes the role originally handled by Miss Fanny Brough, and contrives to make very acceptable the clever but over-long speeches assigned to it. Mr Waller is

as intense, and Miss West as incisive, as before. Mr Hawtrey has grown into the character he assumes, and makes it "tell" at every turn. Than Mr Bishop's Earl and Mr Brookfield's Valet there could be nothing more neat or welcome. Miss Neilson has never looked more handsome, nor has Miss Millett ever been more happy in picturing a typical English girl. The piece, which is brilliantly written, is no less brilliantly staged.

Whether theatre managers in the West End and New York had understood their audiences when they removed Wilde's name from programmes and playbills we cannot tell, but retaining the name did not seem to diminish public interest in *An Ideal Husband*, and when the play was given for a week at the Grand Theatre, Islington (then considered almost provincial) at the beginning of July, Wilde's name was included in the press advertisements. Two months earlier the Theatre Royal, Bath had included Wilde's name in its press advertisements for the week's run of *A Woman of No Importance*. Elsewhere, newspapers were more squeamish: at the end of July, looking back at dramatic successes in the year so far, the Western Mail (published in Cardiff) referred to the author of *An Ideal Husband* as "that misguided genius, "O.W."".

After Bath, the tour went to Birkenhead, where the "Woman of No Importance" Company was reported to be "again doing excellent business" at the Theatre Metropole. By the middle of June the play was being received "with great enthusiasm" in Worcester.

The managers behind the Islington production were Lewis Waller and H H Morell, the same men who had staged the Haymarket and Criterion productions, and it must have been seen as a risk to put it on so soon and so close to those earlier productions. But as the critic in *The Era* said:

> There are not wanting signs that the puppets of paradox, such as we find the characters of the above play to be, have, like the short oaths spoken of by Bob Acres, had their day. But Islingtonians are scarcely so blasé as West-end audiences and therefore the humour and incident of *An Ideal Husband*, which ran its successful course at the Haymarket and Criterion Theatres a short time since, have been highly appreciated at the Grand during the week.

Although the management was the same, only two members of the original cast made it to Islington: Cosmo Stuart, who was promoted from playing the Viscomte de Nanjac to Lord Goring, and Miss Vane Featherston, who had earlier alternated the parts of Lady Markby and Lady Basildon, now played Mrs Cheveley. Two interesting additions to the cast were, as

Lady Chiltern, Lily Hall Caine, sister of the novelist Hall Caine, and as Lady Basildon, Mabel Beardsley, sister of Aubrey. Mabel was not new to Wilde; she is recorded as having played Lady Stutfield in a production of *A Woman of No Importance* at the Theatre Royal, Preston in October 1894.

Waller and Morell took *An Ideal Husband* on a very limited tour after Islington, but had passed the baton to Charles Hawtrey before the end of the year.

Wilde was not seeing any financial advantage from these performances. Ellmann says that "At the bankruptcy sale of Wilde's effects, Alexander had bought the acting rights to The Importance of Being Earnest and Lady Windermere's Fan"[5], which implies that they became Alexander's in April 1895, when the infamous auction in Tite Street was held. But Alexander bought them from the Official Receiver, which means the sale must have come after Wilde's bankruptcy hearing in Carey Street in November, at which point he already had a lien over royalties from the two plays. As we have seen, Waller and Morell were still owed money for *An Ideal Husband*, presumably because of an advance on royalties.

---

5 *Oscar Wilde*, Richard Ellmann, Hamish Hamilton, 1987, p. 544.

3. 1895 – 1900 AND THE DEATH OF WILDE

On the last Saturday of 1895, *The Graphic* carried a review of 'The Drama' as exemplified by West-End productions of the year. The reviewer did not shrink from including Wilde among the major authors mentioned

> In "An Ideal Husband" … Mr Oscar Wilde achieved popular success through a blend of romantic feeling with idealised characterisation, and characteristic wit with Scribe-like scenic knack; but of much higher artistic value was his fantastic "farce for serious people," "The Importance of Being Earnest." This had a delightful freshness of humour and fancy, and the memory of it makes us deplore the loss of such a talent.

In July 1896, Ada Leverson wrote to More Adey prior to Adey's visit to Wilde in Reading Gaol. She asked for a message to go to Wilde from "Cossie" Gordon-Lennox – also known as Cosmo Stuart, under which name he had played the Viscomte de Nanjac in the original production of *An Ideal Husband*.

> [Cossie] is going out on Monday with the 'Ideal Husband'. He is playing Charles Hawtrey's part [Lord Goring]. Alma Stanley is playing Mrs Cheveley, and it is going to be beautifully dressed, and will be on tour till November, it is under Hawtrey's direction. Cossie also asked me to send through you his best love and to say he felt it a great privilege to be able to play in his beautiful works and he looks forward also to seeing him again. We are going down to see the Ideal Husband at Brighton.[1]

A few days later she was able to tell Adey that "'The Ideal Husband'[sic] went splendidly and was wonderfully well received at Newcastle".

When Charles Ricketts visited Wilde in Reading Gaol in May 1897 he found conversation difficult and soon steered it towards the theatre, noting that *Salome* had recently been produced in Paris, and that *Lady Windermere's Fan* had apparently been on in Richmond, although the date has not been established. Wilde therefore had news of the continued success of his plays, even if he did not benefit financially from their performance.[2]

---

1 *Wonderful Sphinx: the biography of Ada Leverson*, Julie Speedie, Virago Press, 1993, p. 103.

2 *Charles Ricketts: a biography*, J G P Delaney, Oxford University Press, 1990, p. 108.

Cossie was clearly delighted with his reception as Lord Goring and placed an advert in the personal columns of *The Era* on 14 November 1896, which took up an entire column and gave quotes from thirty two local newspapers' reviews of his performance in the role. Gordon-Lennox was already well connected, being the son of a Conservative politician and grandson of the Duke of Richmond, but he secured his place in theatrical royalty in 1898 by becoming the second husband of Marie Tempest. (When Cossie died in 1921, Marie married W Graham Browne, who had been Algernon Moncrieffe in George Alexander's revival of *The Importance of Being Earnest*).

Charles Hawtrey's company had first played *An Ideal Husband* just before Christmas 1895 at the Lyric Theatre, Hammersmith, but the touring history of the play had been complicated, even in the brief time since its first production in the West End in January. Lewis Waller and H H Morell, the management who had staged the production at the Haymarket Theatre, had been credited as the management for a performance in March at the Crystal Palace and for the transfer to the Criterion in April. But in June there was a performance at the Theatre Royal, Margate by the Sarah Thorne Company in which the only original cast member was Cosmo Stuart, now playing Lord Goring for the first time. The Sarah Thorne Company was not a touring company but was a stock company based at the Sarah Thorne Dramatic School in Margate; she had some distinguished alumni and could clearly call on professionals to augment her company. The Waller and Morell Company – sometimes referred to as the Haymarket Company - then put on three more dates, at the Grand Theatre, Islington in July, Morton's Model Theatre in Greenwich in September and Ryde, on the Isle of Wight in October.

Lewis Waller, who had played Robert Chiltern at the Haymarket, maintained his role as manager for these performances, but once *An Ideal Husband* had ended its run at the Criterion he moved effortlessly into a series of West End roles, including, at the very end of 1895, that of Stephen d'Acosta in *A Woman's Reason*, by Charles Brookfield and F C Philips. Brookfield, whose dislike of Wilde had manifested itself in his aid for Queensberry before the trials, wrote or co-wrote a number of plays. This was probably his greatest success as a playwright, running for eighty performances.

Waller was a star, and now only stepped outside the West End occasionally, and only to appear in the largest venues. He had not yet quite reached the height of his fame when women would wear a badge proclaiming "KOW" to denote their membership of the Keen on Waller society, and that, according to Hesketh Pearson, meant he never quite achieved his potential: "the puerile nature of the plays he usually put on, and the adolescent behaviour of his female admirers, prevented many people from appreciating his superb gift as a declaimer of Shakespeare's rhetoric, and frequently exposed him to ridicule."[3]

Although Charles Hawtrey had played Lord Goring at the Haymarket, he was not in the cast when the play was presented by his own company. The only cast member to have appeared at the Haymarket was again Cosmo Stuart as Lord Goring. Alma Stanley played Mrs Cheveley (*The Stage* said she appeared "in her familiar role", but it is not clear when she took over from Florence West, the original Mrs Cheveley); and Constance Collier appeared as the Countess of Basildon. *The Stage* reviewed the three performances at the Lyric in glowing terms:

> The performance was deserving of the very highest praise, for not only did the members of the company, without exception, acquit themselves with marked ability, and bring out with telling effect the many excellent points in the brilliant dialogue, but the dresses were superb, and the staging complete to the minutest detail.

The cast were variously "finished and graceful," "very effective," and "clever and amusing." Frank Fenton's Sir Robert Chiltern "was received with every indication of popular favour," and H J Ford as Phipps "found an opportunity for some excellent business."

There was no curtain raiser, but for two of the three nights

> the performance terminated with a dramatic monologue entitled "Fortune's Fool" by Henry H Hamilton, in which Mr Cosmo Stuart appeared as Philip Cholner[4] [sic]. The reading was marked by a great intensity and dramatic power. The story of a life which was made shipwreck of was well told, and the suicide which brings it to a close, just as happiness was within reach was wonderfully realistic.

When this monologue was first presented at the end of the performance of *An Ideal Husband* at the Haymarket on Thursday, 28 March, *The Era* called it a "curious and somewhat morbid little monologue" but concluded that it was "undoubtedly thrilling, and the curtain drops on a strong situation which is worth waiting for. The time of waiting might be curtailed

---

3 *The Last Actor Managers*, Hesketh Pearson, Methuen, 1950

4 The character was Philip Challoner

a little; and we are inclined to counsel the elision of the song." There is no mention of a song in reviews from the Lyric.

A Woman of No Importance had been touring during 1893 and 1894 and had established itself as a profitable play. In June 1895 a long running legal dispute came to court at the Devon Assizes. Messrs H E and J H Reed, owners of a theatre in Union Street, Plymouth (possibly the Grand) were taking breach of contract action against another Mr Reed, the owner of a theatre in Gloucester, who had promised to bring a touring company to Plymouth in 1893. That company, whose principal actress would have been Mme Nerina, would have taken 55% of the takings, with the Reeds taking the rest. Mr Reed had given two weeks' notice of cancellation and the Reeds had to find a replacement (keeping the theatre dark would have resulted in a loss of £42). The replacement – performing *The Outsider* – led to a larger loss of £42 18s 3d, whereas it had been estimated that Mme Nerina's company would have made a profit of £25. In the week prior to the cancelled engagement, the theatre had hosted *A Woman of No Importance* and the gross receipts had been £310. For some weeks before that there had been losses. The judge awarded the Reeds £42 plus costs.

A Woman of No Importance continued to tour until October 1895. This was under the auspices of the H H Morell and Frederick Mouillot company. Both Morell and Mouillot had been jobbing actors since the 1880s, although neither had been particularly successful; Mouillot played Lord Illingworth in this touring production, and that was possibly his most important role to date. Minnie Mouillot was Lady Hunstanton, although it is not clear what if any relation she was to Frederick. But Morell and Mouillot diversified and, in 1884, when Mouillot was only twenty one, they formed a company and bought the Theatre Royal, Bournemouth.

While Lord Illingworth may have been his biggest part, his most memorable had been in 1887 at the Theatre Royal, Exeter where he spoke the final lines on stage before fire gripped the theatre, killing nearly two hundred people and becoming the worst theatre fire in England. As a survivor reported:

> Between the second and fourth acts I left the theatre. Soon after I returned I saw the drop-scene fall almost on Mr. Mouillot's head as he was speaking his lines. He finished what he had to say after the curtain had passed his face, and remarked to a friend "What a strange thing; I never saw that occur before." At the same moment the curtain came forward with a great puff, and seemed to graze my forehead. I saw at the sides sparks and flames, and heard a crackling.

By the late 1890s they owned eighteen theatres, including the Grand Theatre, Swansea, the Theatre Royal, Dublin, the Queen's Opera House, Crouch End, the Coronet, Notting Hill, and the Grand Pavilion, Boscombe. As *The Era* said, in a piece entitled "A Chat with H H Morell" in November 1899, he and Mouillot

> consequently have a full knowledge of the requirements of the playgoing public in various districts

The number and geographic spread of their theatres enabled them to tour plays on their own circuit rather than rely on bookings from other theatre managers, which were unpredictable. This meant their companies could be retained on a lower wage because of relatively long periods of guaranteed work. *An Ideal Husband* was Morell's first experiment as a West End manager. The partnership with Mouillot continued to stage plays in the West End through 1895 and '96, but after that they concentrated on their regional network and overseas interests. Mouillot had business interests in Australia, South America and South Africa where he was an early investor in cinema as well as touring theatrical companies.

In "A Chat with H H Morell", Morell said of touring

> It is only in London itself that the stock company is possible, and if you think awhile you will remember that it thrives more or less. What of the Lyceum under Sir Henry Irving, the Haymarket under Messrs Harrison and Maude, the St James's under George Alexander, and Her Majesty's under Beerbohm Tree? Are not these more or less stock companies? Of course they are always being altered and augmented as were the old stock companies in the days before my time The provincial playgoer demands novelty, and the class of drama, legitimate or illegitimate, that pleased our forefathers and our grandfathers would not be tolerated now. Nor would the old-fashioned methods of acting. People do not crave for realism so much as naturalism, but they won't stand rant. Just think what a stock company would mean at any ordinary theatre in a big town, when you consider the number and the variety of pieces there are on the road. The number and kind that Mr Mouillot and I have under our control, dramas, comedies, farces, and musical plays. We should want half-a-dozen 'crowds' attached to each theatre at least, because you can't run half-a-dozen companies at once without incurring loss, unless each company is selected to play in each different piece. For instance, we play a tragedy piece or a drama piece one week at, we'll say, the Theatre Royal, Tadpole. The next week we have a musical comedy, the week

after that a farce, and the week after that again a Haymarket comedy. If we engaged the finest company of comedians in the world we should not be able to cast all these plays. We should have to pay a large majority of our stock actors to walk about.

Morell went on to talk about how his provincial touring companies allowed the development of young actors by constantly changing casts in touring companies.

One of the actors whose development seems not to have been helped particularly by Morell's companies was Marmaduke Langdale. He appears to have begun touring with them in 1893, and in the Morell and Mouillot production of *A Woman of No Importance* played Sir John Pontefract and, occasionally, Daubeny. Prior to his engagement he had been in the Benson company; a number of Benson's actors frequented a "dim little Soho restaurant" run by a Polish tailor called Joseph Foltinowicz. This was the restaurant which Ernest Dowson was to call 'Poland', and in which in 1889 he set eyes on the owner's daughter Adelaide, with whom he was to fall in love. Langdale, who was called Marmie by Dowson, became part of the poet's group of friends, including Victor Plarr, Aubrey Beardsley, John Gray, Arthur Moore and Langdale's fellow Bensonian, Lennox Pawle. Through this group he was also to know Wilde, W B Yeats and Arthur Symons. In a letter to Victor Plarr in August 1893 Dowson says:

> The darkness of the unknown has swallowed up Hillier, the provincial stage, Marmie.[5]

Two months later he reported to Plarr

> I went down to see Marmie play at Wimbledon the other day. He was an excellent Ralph Nickleby in a tedious play.[6]

Unfortunately, Langdale's theatrical career doesn't appear to have progressed beyond the round of minor roles in the provinces. But in literature, he became the character 'Archie Longdale' in Dowson and Arthur Moore's novel *Adrian Rome*, and assisted Teixeira de Mattos (who married Lily Wilde after Willie Wilde's death) with translation work.

The provincial critics, for the most part, seemed to have little problem with the play, but in the *Gloucester Citizen* at the end of May 1895, the writer had trouble making up his mind:

---

5 *The Letters of Ernest Dowson*, edited by Desmond Flower and Henry Maas, Cassell, 1967 p. 286.

6 Ibid, p. 296.

The celebrity of the play, the notoriety of the author, and perhaps some curiosity as to what sort of personage a woman of no importance could be, proved too much for the stifling heat of a thunderous summer's evening, and the popular parts of the Gloucester Theatre – the dress circle, as is for some inexplicable reason generally the case, was nearly tenantless – were well patronised last night.

The cast were excellent and, as had been established in an earlier piece, the "general tendency" of the play was for good. But not everything was so:

The ethics of the play we do not here propose to discuss in any detail; but, although it contains much that is mere shoddy, and any amount of absurd, flashy paradox and cheap and nasty cynicism, the obvious insincerity and falsity of which grow wearisome to healthy people, there is a considerable proportion of that which is good and true, genuine and brilliant. The audience last night were not slow to recognise this, and from the commencement to the close laughed and applauded in just the right places.

The "necessary padding" as the writer described the entire cast except for the four principals delivered "themselves of Oscar Wilde's characteristically flippant sentiment and twaddling inanities as though to the manner born".

When Morell and Mouillot's tour of *A Woman of No Importance* finished in October 1895, Minnie Mouillot, who had been playing Lady Hunstanton, moved to George Alexander's company and was to be found in the same month in Manchester playing in four plays, including Henry Arthur Jones's *The Triumph of the Philistines* – the play which had replaced *Earnest* at the St James's earlier in the year. She was in this touring company when they were asked to play *Liberty Hall* for the Queen at Balmoral (see F Kinsey Peile's recollections in chapter 1). When Morell and Mouillot revived *A Woman of No Importance* in 1897, Minnie returned as Lady Hunstanton. She then continued to be praised for what were usually relatively small parts in touring productions (always for Mouillot managements) but changed direction in 1900 when advertisements appeared for "Miss Mouillot's Dramatic Classes" which promised "rehearsals on the Stage of a West-end Theatre" – presumably a Mouillot theatre. A further dramatic turn came in 1908, as reported in the *Sheffield Independent*

The future of the Court Theatre has at last been definitely settled, a lease of that house, around which so many pleasant memories cluster, having just been granted by Mr J H Leigh to Miss Mouillot, the principal of the Dramatic Conservatoire, who has long been known as an earnest worker in the domain of the drama.

Lady Windermere's Fan had toured almost from its first performance, but was not touring in 1895, with the exception of a week at the Metropole Theatre in Camberwell in February. This meant that technically Wilde had three plays running in London at the same time for about three days.

In August 1896 George Alexander advertised that the provincial acting rights for seven plays were available: *Dr Bill, The Idler, Lady Windermere's Fan, Liberty Hall, The Masqueraders, The Importance of Being Earnest* and *The Divided Way*. The first touring production of *Lady Windermere's Fan* following Wilde's imprisonment began in October 1896, probably at Colchester. This was staged by the Paula Myrlyn Company, which, over the previous year or so had been touring *Silver Falls* and *Called Back* with some success. The adverts for the second point of call – Ipswich – proclaimed "Miss Paula Myrlyn and Specially Selected London Company in the New and Original Play in Four Acts entitled:- "Lady Windermere's Fan" From the St James's Theatre, London, by Special Arrangement with Geo. Alexander Esq. Prices 6d to 3s 6d." Myrlyn had the courage or foolishness to play the single play for six nights in each venue.

Paula Myrlyn took the part of Mrs Erlynne and *The Era* damned with faint praise – she "gave evidence (more particularly in the testing passage in the third act) of talent as an actress, though her enunciation was not quite so good as one might have anticipated." Maude Paget as Lady Windermere "gained in animation as the evening advanced"; George H Harker as Lord Windermere "was very capable" and William Seguin as Lord Darlington "was equal to what was required from him, which was not very much." As the tour, which was a short one, progressed, Myrlyn's reviews improved. It is not clear whether the tour went on beyond December, when they played in Great Yarmouth, but by June 1897 Paula Myrlyn was advertising in the small ads in *The Era* as "disengaged, heavy lead, offers invited" and was still doing so throughout the rest of the year, thus demonstrating the precarious nature of the profession.

Myrlyn (or Merlyn – even her own publicity was confused about the spelling) took her touring seriously. The advertisement for her tour of *Called Back* advised potential bookers that her company had:

> Twelve kinds of Window Bills, Pictorial and Letterpress. Various Circulars and Throwaways. All the above is Entirely New, and printed by Culliford and Sons in their latest American Style.

Scenery carried: Kenyon's Villas (Built Scene), revolves to Attic; Siberian Prison and Villa on Lake Geneva, by Walter Drury.

Entirely New Wardrobe as used at the Haymarket Theatre.

Lady Windermere's Fan did not tour again until 1899, although there were two one-off performances before then: the first in the Pier Pavilion in Hastings staged by and starring Maurice Bandman. Bandman had been born Maurice E Bandmann in America but dropped the final 'n' as being too Germanic. His fame, which was to come in the next few years, stemmed from his touring overseas and his establishment of a number of theatres, particularly in India. The second was a performance by Nina Cressy's company on the West Pier in Brighton. Cressy's company was a touring one and it may be that this was part of a tour which did not usually feature this play.

The first major tour of *Lady Windermere's Fan* started in late 1899, probably in Llanelli, the company having a number of names: George Alexander's Company, The Elsie Lanham and Alfred Selwyn Company or, most often, The Elsie Lanham Lady Windermere's Fan Company. In some towns they did a split week with *The Importance of Being Earnest*. Elsie Lanham played Gwendolen in this, and Mrs Erlynne in *Lady Windermere*.

When the tour arrived in Oxford, the local press were not impressed

"Lady Windermere's Fan" belongs to the class of society play which is only effective when performed by the best actors and very smartly dressed. The plot is trivial, where it is not impossible, but the dialogue is sparkling and there is a good deal of superficial cleverness about the situations. At the St James's Theatre, with Miss Lily Hanbury in the title role, in the days when the author was seeking popularity as a dramatist, the play made a great success. It is quite a different thing acted and dressed as it was here at the beginning of the week, though the performance possessed merits of its own.

The cast, while well received by most reviewers, did not go on to better things, although Roy Cushing who alternated the parts of Lord Augustus Lorton and Lord Darlington appeared in a silent film in 1925 called *Easy Going Gordon*.

When they played at the Theatre Royal, Hartlepool the play was well received but the occasion was bittersweet:

This the last remaining week of this popular little house's

existence in the dramatic world is one of exceptional attraction, and there are good attendances in all parts of the house to witness the remarkably well finished performance given by Miss Elsie Lanham, Mr Alfred Selwyn and a Co of well chosen artists in Lady Windermere's Fan, The Importance of Being Earnest and Dr Bill.

The Importance of Being Earnest might be expected to have suffered most because of Wilde's downfall, but by October 1895 A B Tapping was touring it with some success, although in an interview in August he had expressed some doubts:

Mr Tapping has, with remarkable audacity, included in his repertory a play by an author whose name is not just now familiar to ears polite; and managers, he is bound to admit, have been rather coy of booking it.

He had three plays in his repertoire for this tour: *Earnest, The Idler*, which Alexander had revived at the St James's in July with several of the original *Earnest* cast, and *Jim the Penman* ("a romance of modern society in four acts") by Sir Charles L Young. *The Idler*, by C Haddon Chambers, had been Alexander's first production as manager at the St James's in 1891 and he had taken it on a provincial tour that year. It was set in fashionable London society and was about gold-diggers. *Jim the Penman*, about a notorious forger, therefore provided a break between two society plays, and Tapping had already played the part of Baron Hartfeld in it over one thousand times.

Tapping had been in the theatre for over thirty years and had strong views about the quality of acting, which he now thought much better than in his early days when he had seen leading men pretend to know roles such as Mark Anthony or Richard III when they had only appeared once in those plays, and then as a young "super". His wife, Florence Cowell, had recently been in America acting in the Kendalls' company but would rejoin his company in a few years. Both of them were active in the welfare of actors and at this time Tapping was on the committees of the Actors' Benevolent Fund and the Royal General Theatrical Fund.

On 12 October the Tapping company reopened the New Alhambra Theatre in Stourbridge ("after a very considerable interval"). Despite whatever misgivings there might have been, when the play then moved to Walsall, the *Walsall Advertiser* was complimentary:

I am glad to see that Mr Tapping thus has the courage to include one of Oscar Wilde's plays in his repertoire.

According to *The Era*, the plays "have all been excellently staged. Mr Tapping's company is in every way first-rate". Of the performance in Limerick, in early November, *The Stage* reported that *Earnest* "attracted the largest house that has been brought together here by a purely dramatic performance since *A Woman of No Importance* was presented by Mr F Mouillot's Co last year".

A Woman of No Importance had not been absent from provincial stages; the Morell and Mouillot tour ended in October 1895 and at the end of February 1896 H W Varna's company opened their tour with it at the Theatre Royal, Bath. It was a short tour of perhaps ten theatres with an additional night in March at the Town Hall in Wells, Somerset. Varna was shortly to become part of Tree's Haymarket Company, playing very minor roles, although that is not obvious from an interview he gave in 1905. Having described his early days as an actor under John S Clarke and several years in the provinces and London stock companies he

> determined that the West End was the goal for me, no matter under what circumstances, and when Mr Tree opened his new theatre in 1897 I was fortunate enough to become engaged by him, and then began the richest experience of my career. I met, in town, all the greatest actors of the day, and observed their work and methods, including Sir Henry Irving [etc., etc.], in fact every artist of note. I met, too, most of the leading playwrights – Henry Arthur Jones, Stephen Phillips, Gilbert and others.

About two years into his time with Tree a vacancy occurred in the "stage-managerial staff"

> Mr Tree knew I had had long experience, and was always attentive to my work and anxious to forge ahead. The proof of this is to be found in the fact that he always entrusted me with parts calling for careful handling. I was, therefore, offered a position on the stage staff, and I gladly accepted it.

He became stage manager at His Majesty's and, when a very "complicated" play was set to tour the colonies he was sent with it. In Australasia he decided to stay, and at the time of this interview was stage manager at a theatre in New Zealand.

Beatrice Homer had played Mrs Allonby in the Morell and Mouillot tour of *A Woman of No Importance* and *The Era* of 31 December 1898 reported that

> Miss Homer now intends to enter into management, and has secured from Mr Beerbohm Tree the rights of the successful

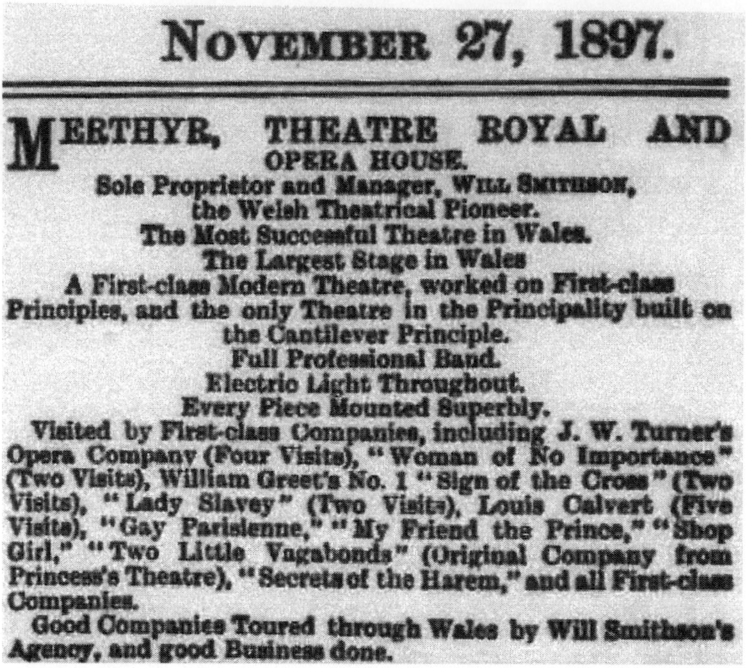

NOVEMBER 27, 1897.

MERTHYR, THEATRE ROYAL AND OPERA HOUSE.
Sole Proprietor and Manager, WILL SMITHSON,
the Welsh Theatrical Pioneer.
The Most Successful Theatre in Wales.
The Largest Stage in Wales
A First-class Modern Theatre, worked on First-class Principles, and the only Theatre in the Principality built on the Cantilever Principle.
Full Professional Band.
Electric Light Throughout.
Every Piece Mounted Superbly.
Visited by First-class Companies, including J. W. Turner's Opera Company (Four Visits), "Woman of No Importance" (Two Visits), William Greet's No. 1 "Sign of the Cross" (Two Visits), "Lady Slavey" (Two Visits), Louis Calvert (Five Visits), "Gay Parisienne," "My Friend the Prince," "Shop Girl," "Two Little Vagabonds" (Original Company from Princess's Theatre), "Secrets of the Harem," and all First-class Companies.
Good Companies Toured through Wales by Will Smithson's Agency, and good Business done.

Fig. 6 Advert for the Theatre Royal, Merthyr Tydfil (from *The Era*, 27 November 1897).

> Haymarket play *A Woman of No Importance*, with which she will open on Boxing Day. Miss Homer will herself sustain the leading role of Mrs Arbuthnot … and as a first-class tour has already been booked and a specially selected company engaged, everything would seem to point to *A Woman of No Importance* being one of the successes of 1899.

This was an interesting piece of placed advertising, as Beatrice Homer's company had been touring *A Woman of No Importance* since June 1898. The performance she gave on Boxing Day was not in a first-class theatre, but in a fit-up venue, the Public Hall in Gravesend. The tour lasted until the end of May 1899, and played over forty venues, but was seen in very few first-class theatres. In September she had advertised

> Towns already Booked: Eastbourne, Swansea (Return), Llanelly, Dudley, Accrington, Bootle, Lancaster (Return), Blackpool (Return), Boscombe, Leigh, Barrow (Return), South Shields (Return), Barrow, West Hartlepool (Return).

Homer was a powerful actor; she had been touring in lead roles for three years, including in Charles Brookfield's *A Woman's Reason*, but had stirred some controversy with her performance in *Woman and Wine* by Benjamin Landeck and Arthur Shirley. When it was revived in the West End at the Princess's Theatre *The Sunday Chronicle*'s critic, while acknowledging that it had had "a perfectly phenomenal success" the previous year, called it "quite an ordinary melodrama, distinguished by a very realistic fight with daggers between two women stripped to the waist". He continued, showing a recognition of the growth of new technology: "There is, in fact, hardly a penny-in-the-slot Cinematograph which does not reproduce the offending incident". In the midst of her *Woman of No Importance* tour, Homer wrote to the editor to complain bitterly as "the original La Colombe in the provinces", and to describe in detail the costumes worn by her and her opponent in the knife fight, thus proving that they were not stripped to the waist. She refers him to the "Mutoscope or, as he designates it, 'the penny-in-the-slot Cinematographe' for verification. Unless his claim was countered she says it would do "an uncalculable amount of harm to an honourable profession".

It was a successful tour. In Swansea in January *The Era* reported that in the previous week "1,787 persons paid for admission to the gallery alone" at the Grand Theatre. In Dudley, Homer recorded "most pleasant recollections of the warm welcome extended to her" in her native town, where her father had been Mayor.

In Accrington it was thought that a "better company of artists could not be wished for," and in Boscombe there was "a good all-round cast". Leyton Cancellor, who had played Mr Kelvil in the Morell and Mouillot tour, was Lord Illingworth, "whose embodiment is highly commendable." Mr Kelvil, "the doctrinaire MP is a capital assumption by Mr W J Butler", indeed, the only member of the cast to receive a less than fulsome description was Herbert Greville who was "quite characteristic as the Venerable Archdeacon Daubeney"; that was ambiguous to say the least. Beatrice Homer's "intensely dramatic and effective representation of the unfortunate heroine, Mrs Arbuthnot, elicits the plaudits of an appreciative audience". Herbert Greville is rarely mentioned in reviews – never getting more than a "satisfactory" - whereas most of the remainder of the cast are noted with approval.

In July the tour arrived in Southport for a week's stay; a local paper demonstrates the competition that touring plays were up against during the holiday season:

> The heavy rain of this week, following the long spell of dry weather, has immensely improved the appearance of the boulevards and the Marine Parks The weather yesterday was

very bright, and as the barometer was steadily rising it promises to be an extremely fine week end. Visitors may possibly miss Signor La Camera's military band, but their place has been taken by the band of the 3rd V.B.K.L.R., by which concerts are given every evening in the North Marine Park. This is followed nightly by a clever entertainment given by the Pierrots, a capable troupe of artistes, who are this year maintaining the success which they achieved last season. At the Pier extensive alterations are contemplated. Some of these have already been carried through. An admirable band has also been engaged, and three concerts are given daily. Sacred concerts are given on Sunday evenings at both the Pier and the Marine Park, and so far these have proved extremely popular. A varied programme is also provided at the Circus and the Winter Gardens. This week at the Opera House "A Woman of No Importance" has drawn good houses, and for next week "Morocco Bound" is underlined. Entertainments are provided at the Botanic Gardens, the Kew Gardens, and the Victoria Baths, while a fine fleet of pleasure boats is available for trips to Llandudno, Blackpool, and other pleasure resorts. In fact, for a week end or a longer stay, Southport presents many attractions just now.

In early February 1900 *The Morning Post* said

On the 19th inst Mrs Lewis Waller will open her spring tour at the Coronet Theatre with a new play, entitled "Tess," by Mr H A Kennedy. Mrs Waller will play the title role, and she will be supported by Miss Mary Rorke, Miss Annie Webster, and Mr William Kittridge. "The Three Musketeers" and "A Woman of No Importance" will be in the repertory during the tour.

Mrs Lewis Waller (Florence West) had performed in *A Woman of No Importance* at the Coronet Theatre in Notting Hill at the end of November 1899 and was to appear in it again at the Theatre Royal, Manchester in March 1900. *The Three Musketeers* had been in her repertory for her autumn tour in 1899, but for the spring tour of 1900 she would appear to have performed only *Tess*, an adaptation by the American Kennedy of Thomas Hardy's novel *Tess of the d'Urbervilles*. While garnering some praise, particularly for the staging, the majority of reviews found *Tess* unsatisfactory, with *The Standard* saying that the author "succeeded in retaining a great deal of the story's dramatic interest" but that at the same time he had "retained its gloomy tragedy, and this on the stage becomes sordid and almost repulsive."

The Standard had also been uncomplimentary about the performance of *A Woman of No Importance* at the Coronet, although the critic notably

Fig. 7 *Woman of No Importance*, Coronet Theatre, Notting Hill, 1899. RHC RW/11/1/3/4 RHUL Archives.

65

acknowledged that the author was Oscar Wilde. He thought the revival

> cannot be regarded with satisfaction by the well-wishers of
> the drama. It is one of the most immoral examples of the series
> of marriage-problem plays which a few years ago obtained
> ephemeral popularity. Its chief objectionableness is not in its trite
> and unpleasant story, but in the specious glitter of its dialogue
> in which the principles of true happiness and nobility of life are
> derided with covert sneer. Fortunately the singular unreality
> and insincerity of the work are so patent that the falseness of its
> philosophy must be apparent to the majority of spectators; but
> it is not by the performance of such works that respect will be
> increased for English drama.

Nevertheless, at least one paper reported in May that "there is some talk" of a London revival of "the clever comedy" *A Woman of No Importance*, with Mr and Mrs Lewis Waller. A few days later we were told that Mrs Beerbohm Tree had been offered her old part in the revival, which "is intended only for a series of matinees," and would therefore not interfere with her evening engagements. The revival did not happen and, in any case, in the same month *The Era* carried the announcement that

> Miss Beatrice Homer has secured from Mr Beerbohm
> Tree, for an indefinite period, the rights of "A Woman of No
> Importance" and will start her second tour of same on July 9th,
> running through the autumn and into 1901, and visiting most
> of the principal towns.

This she did; in December *The Era* claimed that the piece had been "rebooked at every theatre visited, only four spring dates being left vacant". The tour finished in June 1901.

In February 1900 Nina Cressy's Company began a tour in which both *Lady Windermere's Fan* and *An Ideal Husband* were announced as in repertory. However, only two bookings for the former have been found – at Margate and Hastings – before her choice of Wilde play turned to *An Ideal Husband*, which she toured throughout the summer and autumn. In Margate, Arthur Wontnor revelled "in the mixture of severity and dignity desirable in the successful delineation of the part of Lord Windermere," and "Too much cannot be said in favour of Miss Nina Cressy's acting as Mrs Erlynn". The play was performed on the Monday and Tuesday, with the second play – *The Profligate* – playing on Wednesday. Thursday "was a grand fashionable night, under the patronage of the Mayor, and at which between act three and four of "Lady Windermere's Fan" a tableau representing "Our Home and Colonial Forces" was introduced, and wherein

Councillor Hughes recited the patriotic address, "Ordered to the Front."

The reason for abandoning *Lady Windermere's Fan* is not clear, although *An Ideal Husband* had not toured for a while and therefore had novelty value. The actor playing Lord Windermere was J Cooke Beresford, although he does not make an appearance in *An Ideal Husband*. He had begun acting in 1890 and performed small parts in a number of Shakespeare plays at the Olympic Theatre in London during 1892; according to his professional biography he was in South Africa at the time of the Jamieson Raid and was a member of the Australian Brigade under Wools Sampson and "Karri" Davies.

An Ideal Husband toured in repertory with *The Professor's Love Story* by J M Barrie and *Moths*, an adaptation of Ouida's novel of the same name. These were very popular plays; when Barrie's play had first been produced in the West End in 1894, two new rows of stalls had to be installed.

Lady Windermere's Fan reappeared at the end of 1900 under the management of T B Thalberg. J Cooke Beresford must have impressed in the Cressy production because, although Thalberg took the part of Lord Windermere for himself, Beresford was now cast as Lord Darlington. But the big draw for this production was the appearance of Marion Terry as Mrs Erlynne. She had played the part in the original production in 1892 at the St James's Theatre, and was the sister of Ellen Terry – a member of one of the greatest acting dynasties of the age.

The company was alternating *Lady Windermere's Fan* with *The School for Scandal* and *Queen o'Scots*; in these latter two Marion Terry played Lady Teazle – a part new to her – and Queen Mary. She got good notices in each of the plays, but as Mrs Erlynne

> The charm of her presence, the easy grace of her bearing, her outbursts of passion, her steady, cool nonchalance – all these, with an ever present halo of sympathetic womanliness, make this one of Miss Terry's most successful artistic efforts.

The tour started at Kennington at the Princess of Wales's Theatre where, it was noted,

> [t]he author's name was duly mentioned on the bills outside the theatre, but on the programme 'discreet silence' was preserved as to the fact that *Lady Windermere's Fan* was from the brilliant pen of Oscar Wilde. Surely a man should receive credit for his work, even if he be dragging out his existence under a cloud; if his play is good enough to perform, so certainly he ought to be named as author.

The same reviewer, in *The Stage*, was ambivalent about Marion Terry's performance, saying that she

> has latterly been seen more often in the stalls on "first nights" than on the boards, and hence even her passing re-appearance in London is a matter for more than ordinary satisfaction. Obviously very nervous on Monday, and relying a good deal on the obtrusive aid of a loud-voiced prompter, Miss Marion Terry repeated her admirable embodiment of an almost heartless woman

Thalberg's real name was Corbett, but he had adopted the name of his godfather, the pianist Sigismund Thalberg as a nom de théâtre. He had acted in stock companies and provincial touring companies and performed regularly in the West End throughout the 1890s. He also spent time in America, acting opposite Madame Modjeska in many productions.

The end of the century also saw a major step on the road to Wilde's full theatrical rehabilitation with the first amateur productions. On 4 and 5 December 1899 the George Alexander Dramatic Club presented, as their seventh annual production, *Lady Windermere's Fan* at the Athenaeum Theatre, Glasgow. They were a little fettered in their choice of material because, as they were under the patronage of George Alexander, they put on only plays in his repertoire, but nevertheless this may have been considered a bold choice. If the reviewers thought so they overlooked the fact

> Last night the performance went with the utmost smoothness from the opening to the final fall of the curtain. The amateur aspect was not wholly absent, but the acting of Mr Stanley Harrison as Lord Windermere and of Mr Sam Shields as Lord Augustus Lorton made amends for any apparent defects on the part of others.

Elsie Lanham's company performed the same play at the same theatre less than two weeks later.

In February 1900 The Bancroft Dramatic Club, who clearly did not owe the same allegiance to their patron as those supported by George Alexander, also performed *Lady Windermere's Fan*. This was at St George's Hall, Langham Place in London and *The Morning Post* printed the full cast list, something it rarely did for professional productions, and claimed that they

> brought once more before us one of the wittiest and best written comedies of our times ... rarely have the efforts of amateurs proved more satisfactory and successful. Non-

professional ladies and gentlemen are seen at their best in society plays, in which a faithful reproduction of contemporary manners is the chief requisite. But they are terribly handicapped by our recollection of the first-rate companies to whom we owe the original presentation of these pieces. The Bancroft Club last night almost succeeded in banishing these importunate memories.

Finally, on the day before Wilde died, there was an amateur performance of *Lady Windermere's Fan* in the Opera House and Winter Gardens in Southport, a theatre in which Wilde had lectured three times.

Local newspapers around the country reported the death of Wilde and his funeral. The tone was different for each: his death was the opportunity to list his works and his educational achievements but not to dwell on the reason he was in Paris at the end. Perhaps *The Manchester Courier* spoke for other newspapers when it said

> The circumstances of the scandal which consigned him to a gaol and to oblivion, are too recent and too horrible to need recapitulation.

When reporting his funeral, however, there is a sadness at the lowly and lonely end of the writer.

4. ANTIPODEAN INTERLUDES

Australia seems to have been particularly keen on Wilde. On 14 January 1895, less than two weeks after its first performance, the *Morning Post* and other papers reported that "Mr Oscar Wilde has already had offers to produce his play [*An Ideal Husband*] in America, Australia, Berlin, Vienna and Sweden". When lecturing in America in 1882, Wilde had said that he planned to go to Japan and Australia and, at the time of his trials one New South Wales paper reported that

> At one time he was arranging with Mr R S Smythe to tour Australia as one of that gentleman's gallery of "celebrities"

Two months after the play's opening in London, on 17 March 1895, the Sydney *Sunday Times* printed an interview with Dion Boucicault in which he told them that the current "Brough and Boucicault season at the Lyceum will close with Oscar Wilde's new and original four-act play of modern life, 'An Ideal Husband'". The season had started on 9 March with Henry Arthur Jones's *The Masqueraders*. The piece went on to say that "the firm's London representative, Mr Charles Cartwright, has cabled out the intelligence that he has secured for them Wilde's latest play, "The Importance of Being Earnest."

In *An Ideal Husband*, George Titheradge, one of the country's favourite actors, would play Sir Robert Chiltern.

As with the London press, the Wilde trials caught the Australians unprepared. But unlike London, Australia relied on two major forms of communication to find out about what was happening in Britain: telegraph and mail ships. This led to some quite virulent reporting of the trial – particularly the libel trial – running alongside articles describing the fashions in *The Importance of Being Earnest* at the St James's Theatre.

The coverage of the trial was not sympathetic to Wilde; the *Clarence and Richmond Examiner* in New South Wales nailed its colours to the mast with

> The Wilde-Queensberry sensation is the most revolting one of the century, not even excepting Mr Stead's "Maiden Tribute" disclosures in the *Pall Mall Gazette*. … As for Oscar Wilde, I once met him at the Lotus Club in New York. He struck me as a large, raw-boned person, with a face like a horse, and an insolent bearing.

A newspaper called *Truth*, in Sydney, ran a piece under the heading "Oscar Wilde: the Beauteous and the Buoyant; The Arsenal of Aestheticism":

> The aesthetic poet of the langorous city of soulless love, the lover of everything limp, spineless, delicate and untouchable, has fallen in. He who could lunch on the smell of a lily, and would faint at the sight of a boiled carrot, has been adjudicated by the Court to be something lower than the beasts of the field: a creature for whose peculiar offending in Australia the lash would be the punishment. He charged the Marquis of Queensberry with libelling him. But the Marquis proved the poet was a libertine of the worst type – a man unfitted for association with any but the vilest of his fellows – one of that peculiarly constituted section of humanity for whose offence Sodom was destroyed and Gomorrah burned with fire from Heaven. Oscar Wilde was one of those implicated in the Cleveland-street Scandals years ago, and only escaped prosecution by the merest accident. He has since been arrested and will be criminally charged.

This was even before the two criminal trials. Other papers took a more pragmatic view:

> So far as we may speculate on futurity, it seems that Oscar Wilde has closed a career of bizarre brilliance.

> His later plays … would doubtless have reached this city [Adelaide] in due course, but whether they will do so now seems uncertain.

The second quote above is from an article headed "Erratic, Erotic".

An Ideal Husband opened at the Lyceum Theatre in Sydney on Saturday 13 April 1895, while Wilde was in Holloway following his arrest. According to the *Sunday Times* it

> went well, and there was a call at the end of each act …. If admirable staging and acting, and smart dialogue count for anything Oscar Wilde's brilliant play should crowd the Lyceum all the week.

Others reported that there was a full house and that the play was "a decided success"; *Truth*, while claiming that "In America they have started burning [Wilde's] books" reviewed the play well, saying that

> Mr Titheradge was so earnest, so faithfully artistic and perfectly natural, as to make his Sir Robert Chiltern an especially convincing character and one towards whom an instinctive wave of sympathy was almost inconsciously [sic] directed.

But there was no getting away from the author's troubles. The Sydney *Evening News* summed the situation up thoughtfully

> With respect to the latest production of the Brough and Boucicault Company and, according to announcement, the final one of the season – there are, as most people are doubtless aware, very special reasons indeed for remembering that, after all, "the play's the thing." As compared with his work, the author is but a secondary consideration, or at least should be under ordinary conditions. However in this case it would be the silliest of affectations to ignore the fact that most of those who went to the Lyceum on Saturday evening to see "An Ideal Husband" must have had in their minds certain recent disclosures with respect to the writer of the piece too fearfully irreconcilable with ideal standards of any kind. Let this suffice in the way of allusion to the moral problems involved, and as to the question of the taste and judgment displayed by the management. If they were influenced, as they probably were, by the consideration that the piece would prove a draw, the result so far justified their decision. The house was very full …

Brough and Boucicault had of course acquired the rights to *An Ideal Husband* before Wilde's legal problems became known, and while the expectation of prurience among the audience may well have influenced their decision to go ahead with the play, it was clearly a gamble which came off. What appears to be a lone voice of protest was raised in *Table Talk*, a Melbourne paper:

> One cannot help feeling some disgust in noticing that a play of Oscar Wilde's is acted in Sydney. Can not this reptile be stamped out utterly? What do we want with plays written by the Devil? To be sure managers are disastrously affected by having given long prices for *Lady Windermere's Fan*, *The Importance of Being Earnest*, *A Woman of No Importance* and *An Ideal Husband*, and certain it is they will never get the money back, play or no play.

At this time, only *An Ideal Husband* and *Lady Windermere's Fan* had been seen in Australia.

The final performance of *An Ideal Husband* in Sydney was on 21 April when "a cordial and exceedingly large audience crowded the Lyceum … The curtain finally fell amidst prolonged enthusiasm, but no speeches were made." The papers here and elsewhere on the tour noted that the dress-circle was unusually full, which led one commentator to wonder whether the "fashionable folk" might not have "as high a standard of morality as they ought to possess" because they had only gone to see the play "because the author has proved himself to be a most abominable sinner". The same commentator gave the play a reasonable review.

Brough and Boucicault then moved to Brisbane at the beginning of May, where both *An Ideal Husband* and *Lady Windermere's Fan* were performed at the Opera House. The adverts were able to announce

> By the courtesy of the Railway Commissioners, the 11.15pm Train to Sandgate will stop at Wooloowin and Albion during the Brough-Boucicault Season.

An Ideal Husband was performed in Newcastle on 22 May and then the Company moved to Melbourne at the beginning of June. The first play in the season was Henry Arthur Jones's *The Case of Rebellious Susan*, which seems not to have been to Melbourne's taste, and then on 8 June, *An Ideal Husband* – announced as "by the author of Lady Windermere's Fan". This led one paper to describe the decision not to name Wilde as "cant":

> If the man's plays are playable (and nobody has, so far as we know, discovered anything wrong in them) why resort to the policy of ignoring the name of the author? Mr Sydney Grundy has given his opinion on this matter, as a brother dramatist. "I wonder," says he, "on what principle of law, or justice, or common sense, or good manners, or Christian charity, an author's name is blotted from his work. If a man is not to be credited with what he has done well, by what right is he punished for what he has done ill?" Surely this is a sensible as well as a fair play argument …. Even devils have their rights.

On 3 August, the Melbourne paper *The Argus* carried an advert announcing that, on 10 August, for the "First Time in Australia" *The Importance of Being Earnest* would be performed. The advert gave the play's subtitle, but failed to make any mention of an author. There was disagreement as to its popularity. *The Argus* said

> In the estimation of a large audience, as testified by the abundance of its laughter and the frequency and heartiness of its applause, "The Importance of Being Earnest" is one of the most successful productions of the Brough and Boucicault season.

Table Talk thought that "the audience are kept in a simmer of merriment all the time", and *The Australasian* reported a large audience. But *Australian Town and Country* (admittedly published in Sydney rather than Melbourne) was convinced that the play "has not pleased the people here". *The Stage's* Australian correspondent reported that, despite some fine acting,

> The wondrously sustained brilliancy and verbal sparkle of

"The Importance of Being Earnest" failed to compensate for the antipodean prejudice in regard to its authorship. Melbourne society would have none of it.

This sounds very much like playing to the London readership. Melbourne society, as in other Australian cities, couldn't get enough.

The apparent lack of an author was addressed

A cynic in the gallery at the Melbourne Princess Theatre a few evenings since, at the conclusion of the performance of "The Importance of Being Earnest," raised a call for 'author!' The cry was taken up by a group who seemed to find some humor in it. The author did not make his appearance. In fact, if one goes by the programmes, play-bills, and advertisements, the piece never had an author. It seems, like Topsy, to have 'growed.'

The main concern of the Australian press was an attempt to explain the play to its readers. *The Argus* admitted that it was "a piece very difficult of classification, but there is very little uncertainty as to its parentage" and when it opened in Adelaide in early September, the *Quiz and Lantern* tried to help its readers:

No doubt you are wondering what on earth "The Importance of Being Earnest" is about. Its author is at work upon physical gymnastics and not literary topsy-turvydoms, so you need not bother about him. Well, it is an attempt on the part of the late socially lamented Oscar to satirise society in Gilbertian fashion, and is brilliant, piquant, artificial, and innocent. A strange dramatic *pot pourri* from such a pen, but so it is. You may all take your grandparents to it; though don't take the children – they may prefer something more (Sarah) Grand and Ibsen(e).

The South Australian Register demonstrated a strong grasp neither of the play, nor of the English language

It resembles a tasty dish so savoury that one would not like to be disillusionized. It might be fricasseed frogs' legs, guineapigs' tails, or a symphony in pigs' trotters, but it is nice, and all the nicer for the mystery.

From Adelaide the company sailed across to New Zealand, beginning a short tour in Auckland and then travelling to Wellington. They did not take *Earnest* on this tour, but staged *An Ideal Husband*. In Wellington it was said

If the Auckland Brough and Boucicault season was one big success, then the Wellington season was a bigger success. This week our Governor, Lord Glasgow, and party have attended four performances out of six.

A three night season in Wanganui did not include a Wilde play, but *An Ideal Husband* was back in the repertory for Christchurch in early December.

Although it was the Brough and Boucicault Company, Robert Brough and his wife had left Australia for England in March, returning only for the start of the company's Sydney season which began on Boxing Day with Henry Arthur Jones's *The Amazons*. This tour was advertised as marking the termination of the partnership and included *An Ideal Husband* and *The Importance of Being Earnest*. In the former there was disagreement as to whether Mrs Brough was an improvement over Geraldine Olliffe as Mrs Cheveley. Through much of 1896 the tour followed the same course as the previous year, but with the termination of their partnership, Dion Boucicault backed out and Robert Brough formed the Brough Comedy Company. On 2 January 1897 the *Sydney Morning Herald* carried an advert for the performance the following week of

> First production in Australia of the Famous Play by Oscar Wilde, author of "An Ideal Husband," "The Importance of Being Earnest," "Lady Windermere's Fan," &c entitled "A Woman of No Importance"

Given its popularity in British theatres it is odd that *A Woman of No Importance* should have been the last of the four comedies to reach Australia, although there seems to have been some confusion because several press reports referred to it as Wilde's "latest play". The inclusion of Wilde's name in the adverts drew praise from *Truth* – a paper which had not always been sympathetic:

> In staging the best and latest play of a once popular but now degraded and despised genius, Oscar Wilde, they have started honestly by acknowledging the name and authorship of the fallen dramatic genius and dethroned social idol. This is not merely magnanimous; it is much more. If a man's name is not fit to be mentioned, the fruit of his genius ought not to be fit for representation. Oscar Wilde's sins may have ruined him and tarnished his name and fame, but they can never extinguish the bright scintillations of pathos, wit and humor which sparkle and scintillate throughout his plays, and above all in "A Woman of No Importance"

A week later the same paper considered the play "stands conspicuously above "The Second Mrs Tanqueray", and believed that, whatever his defects, Wilde's "writings belong to the century."

Some had been concerned that a light comedy called *Nancy & Co* was

Plate 1 *The Importance of Being Earnest* Coronet Theatre, Notting Hill, 1901.
Private Collection.

Plate 2. One of a pair of posters for *A Woman of No Importance* (probably 1898).
Private Collection.

Plate 3. One of a pair of posters for *A Woman of No Importance* (probably 1898).
Private Collection.

Plate 4. *An Ideal Husband*, New Theatre, Cambridge, 1905. Private Collection.

withdrawn to make way for *A Woman of No Importance*, but Robert Brough made clear that runs of individual plays had to be kept short in order to meet contractual requirements which promised British rights holders a number of performances. Later he would state that no run should last longer than twelve days. After a very successful run in Sydney, *A Woman of No Importance* was itself withdrawn in favour of *A Woman's Reason* by Charles Brookfield and F C Phillips. On the last night of Wilde's play in Sydney there was "an audience that packed every portion of the auditorium" and it was hailed as "one of the most successful 'runs' on record".

When the play opened in Melbourne in the first week of February, "no reception could have been more hearty". It was again followed by Brookfield's play but clearly missed:

> Mr Brough intends to try a number of revivals when "A Woman's Reason" has run its course …. But this many playgoers would cheerfully dispense with in favour of a few extra nights of "A Woman of No Importance"

Their wish was granted when it was "revived for three nights only" before going on to Brisbane. Here it was only intended to play it for two nights but again there was pressure to revive it and Brough did so on 7 May "positively this night only".

Critics generally thought *A Woman of No Importance* to be Wilde's best play, taking that position from *Lady Windermere's Fan*. One thought there had been "no keener satire on 'society'" since *School for Scandal*. It is not clear that all of them understood the humour; a critic in *The Australasian* said

> Some of the women of more or less importance in this play, as in other plays by the same author, give one the impression that while they express the ideas of an advanced barmaid deprived of their barbaric ruggedness by the glamour of cultivated speech, they don't really mean what they say, and are only "showing off" in what a cyclist would describe as a conversation highly geared.

After Brisbane the company returned to Sydney where there was a "farewell benefit and public testimonial" for Mr and Mrs Brough to mark the end of a twelve year association with the city. There was a short season in Adelaide, followed by seventeen nights in August in Wellington (it is not clear whether other parts of New Zealand were visited on this tour). The Broughs then set off for other parts of the British Empire after which the company was dissolved.

A Woman of No Importance was not performed again in Australia within our period, although it clearly left an impression, as evidenced by a poorly informed writer in *Table Talk* in 1902

> The only play of the gifted and ill-starred author that has been produced in Melbourne is *A Woman of No Importance*, which is the most brilliant comedy of modern times that Melbourne has ever seen.

Despite the tearful farewells to the Broughs, they were back in 1900. For this tour, which started as usual in Sydney, *An Ideal Husband* was nominally in the repertory but they seem only to have played it in Brisbane and Perth, where the advertising was able to claim that it was

> The First Production in Western Australia

The local press greeted their arrival with facts and figures:

> upwards of 150 tons of scenery, furniture and stage properties will arrive here on Thursday by the Pilbarra. The company consists of 26 people

The six week Perth season started on 6 September and, at the end, somewhat surprised by the company's success, Brough announced that they would come back after their planned two week season in Kalgoorlie (where Wilde was not performed). When they returned, *An Ideal Husband* played for three of the eight nights and the Theatre Royal was "well filled".

Oddly, although *Lady Windermere's Fan* had been a favourite in Australia, there was no further professional production during our period. It did, however, become a staple of two well-known amateur companies: The Appendreena Club, based in Adelaide, performed it in 1905 and twice in 1906, and The Players performed it in the same years in Melbourne and Sydney.

Similarly, *The Importance of Being Earnest* became a popular play for amateur companies. The Idlers Dramatic Club played it in Sydney in 1904 (where Mrs John Lemmone, as Lady Bracknell, "handled her muff most daintily"), and the following year an amateur company in Hobart performed this "clever and amusing comedy" but, unusually by this time failed to mention the author. The Appendreena Club played it in 1906; in 1907 the Sydney University Dramatic Society's production had Governor Rawson in the audience and his youngest son in the cast; and in 1908 the Cottesloe Dramatic Society in Perth performed under the patronage of the Governor and Lady Bedford. The play appears only to have been played professionally twice more in our period, by the Brough Company in 1902 in Kalgoorlie and Perth.

Although Australia and New Zealand were at the heart of the Brough and Boucicault Company, and afterwards the Brough Comedy Company, each year saw them take their repertory to other destinations. From Australia they would normally go to India and to China and Singapore. It is not clear whether there was a tour in India, or simply a season in Calcutta. Certainly the company performed *An Ideal Husband* there in early 1897 and *The Importance of Being Earnest* at the end of the year and into 1898, along with *Lady Windermere's Fan*. The local paper, the *Englishman*, said of *Earnest* that it was "beautifully mounted, and most sympathetically treated by a cast who knew exactly how to give point to the phenomenal brilliancy of the dialogue ….. The enormous house was transported, and the curtain had to be twice raised at the end of each act".

In 1901 the *Stage* reported

> For the last five weeks the Lyceum, Shanghai has been nightly crowded by enthusiastic audiences to witness the excellent performances of the Brough Comedy company under the direction of Mr Robert Brough. They came on here from Calcutta, after a most successful season there, and opened at the Lyceum with "The Liars," in which they showed conclusively to Shanghai that they could not only act, but act admirably. … The next visit of this company is already being looked forward to by Shanghailanders. The Broughs have now gone to Hong Kong, from which they proceed to Australia.

There were fourteen plays, including *An Ideal Husband* in the repertory for Shanghai.

The Broughs toured South Africa later in their career, but in 1897 *Lady Windermere's Fan* was taken there by Herbert Flemming and his company. They sailed from Southampton on the SS Tartar at the end of March with "elaborate properties and wardrobe" on board. On the way they gave a performance on board – it is not clear which play was given – the proceeds from which, a total of £17 2s, were split equally between the Actors' Benevolent Fund and the seamen's widows and orphans. The first stop was Port Elizabeth where they played for nine nights; *Lady Windermere's Fan* was one of six plays performed. The company then moved to Kimberley and Natal, where they were voted "the best company that has visited the Colonies". There was some confusion in the reviews as *Lady Windermere's Fan* was said to have "Mr Flemming in the title role". From Natal they moved to Durban where the play opened "to a full house, and scored an instantaneous success".

Flemming's company left Durban after a four week season, travelling through East London, King Williamstown, Port Elizabeth and opening in Johannesburg in September. There they played at the Standard Theatre, which Flemming had secured at what was seen as the favourable rate of £400 a month for ten weeks. They opened with *Lady Windermere's Fan* "to a moderately good house," but "business rose every night, until on the Saturday Mr Flemming had to refuse money in all parts".

Flemming remained in South Africa, managing a circuit of ten theatres, until the outbreak of the Boer War in 1899, when he returned to England. In 1902 he went to Australia, where he formed a partnership with Robert Brough and the company toured India and South Africa.

Brough died in 1905; his obituary in *The Church Commonwealth* said that he

> did for Australia what Henry Irving did for England in making the theatre a respectable institution

Flemming died in 1908, having acted to within two months of his death.

5. BACK IN THE WEST END

We have seen that during our period all four of the comedies played at what would today be considered inner London theatres. If we include some slightly further out, the metropolis had been effectively ringed by productions by the time the first West End revival took place.

South of the Thames the plays had been seen in Greenwich, Camberwell, Kennington and at the Elephant and Castle. North of the river they had been produced in Hammersmith, Islington, Holloway, Ealing, Kilburn, Crouch End, Notting Hill and Camden Town. Sometimes the theatrical papers reviewed these as London theatres, sometimes they were classified as provincial. The theatres definitely thought of themselves as being London theatres. The Coronet Theatre in Notting Hill proudly advertised itself as "The only theatre on the Central London Railway", and elsewhere adverts trumpeted the benefits of attending a local theatre when thick fog was prevalent in the centre of London.

Nevertheless, the true reclamation of Wilde as a playwright could not begin until at least one of his plays had been produced again in the West End.

Ironically, the first Wilde play to make it to the West End after 1895 was one he had not written. On 25 October 1900 at the Royalty Theatre in Dean Street, Mrs Patrick Campbell opened in *Mr and Mrs Daventry*, "A New and Original Play, in Four Acts, by Frank Harris". This was the play Harris had written based on a scenario which he had purchased from Wilde, probably in late 1899. Harris was to find to his cost once rehearsals were announced that he was not the only one who had paid for the scenario: Charles Frohman, Ada Rehan, Horace Sedger, Cora Brown-Potter and Louis Nethersole also claimed ownership.[1]

Although among Wilde's friends the genesis of the play was well-known, it is probably fortunate for Wilde's rehabilitation that the press failed to find out. If they had, the reviews might have contained even worse than they did. *The Era*, two days after the opening, carried one of the kinder reviews which began:

---

1 *Oscar Wilde*, Richard Ellmann, Hamish Hamilton, 1987 p. 544 and *Additions and Corrections to Richard Ellmann's* Oscar Wilde, Horst Schroeder, The Author, 2nd edition 2002, pp. 211-12.

Mr and Mrs Daventry is certainly not the sort of play to which to take the typical young lady of seventeen. Indeed, some adult, but old-fashioned, playgoers may, perhaps, find the picture it gives of a certain phase of life rather too boldly drawn. But if one can stand the realism of certain scenes and excuse the strained style of the lighter dialogue, Mr Frank Harris's play makes the inevitable appeal of the "naked truth," as one of the minor characters in the cast puts it.

Max Beerbohm and J T Grein gave the play positive reviews, but for the most part the reviews followed the lines of the *Leeds Times* – "a clever but not pleasant study of an unhappy marriage," or the *Newcastle Courant* – "It is a pity that so much excellent work from all concerned has been lavished upon a play the moral tone of which is so daring that one wonders how it has ever managed to pass the censor". The crowds still came, partly because, in the words of the *Gloucester Journal* it was a "naughty but very successful play which everybody goes to see in order to judge whether it is really as bad as everybody says it is."

Nevertheless, some toning down was called for and the *Newcastle Courant* seemed conflicted in reporting on 1 December:

Mrs Patrick Campbell has induced Mr Max Beerbohm to dramatise his dainty little allegorical story, "The Happy Hypocrite," which she purposes playing in front of "Mr and Mrs Daventry." This latter play has had much of the more objectionable matter deleted [from the first act], though there still remains a good deal that would have been better never written. It is thoroughly well played and is still drawing crowded houses.

Perhaps they were also coming to see the theatre, which it was reported Mrs Patrick Campbell had requested be repainted "a soft shade of green".

Charles Ricketts saw it on 6 November and recorded in his journal:

Went to the Oscar-Harris play, found it curiously, quite nakedly direct, not one word that was not necessary to the business; certainly the most crude and telling play I have seen on the English stage, hence all the howls in the press over bad construction, superfluous dialogue, bad epigrams, etc., etc, This play of four acts takes about one hour and a half to act. I was interested in the audience of well-bred men and vulgar women, such as you see at the Savoy Restaurant. I wonder if all smart women are vulgar? The audience simmered with delight, but did not applaud.[2]

---

2 *Self Portrait: Taken from the Letters and Journals of Charles Ricketts, R A,*

After a two week interruption to mark the death of Queen Victoria, *Mr and Mrs Daventry* celebrated its 100th performance on 5 February 1901, but closed less than three weeks later, on 23 February after a total of 121 performances. It was not performed again until a radio adaptation was broadcast in 1955.

Plays actually written by Wilde, however, were getting ever closer to the West End.

In November 1901, George Alexander had started a short tour of *The Importance of Being Earnest* at the Theatre Royal, Manchester. He then took it to Belfast, Dublin and Nottingham before testing the metropolitan audience at the Coronet Theatre in Notting Hill; then to the Theatre Royal in Brighton, where he and other companies had previously visited during runs in London. Finally, on 16 December, the play came to South London at the Kennington Theatre.

With the new year, adverts started to appear announcing the last performances of *The Wilderness* by H. V. Esmond (a play which had run for fourteen weeks from 11 April and subsequently toured successfully) and that "The Importance of Being Earnest (By the Author of Lady Windermere's Fan) will be revived for a limited number of performances on Tuesday Evening, Jan 7th, at 8.45. Preceded at 8 by A Patched-up Affair by Florence Warden". The inclusion of *Earnest* in the St James's season seems to have been a late decision. A.E.W. Mason, in his early history of Alexander and the St James's Theatre says of the tour:

> He had never had a doubt that a time would come, and within a reasonable period, when this iridescent bubble of gaiety and wit would dance in the air again to the delight of all men's ears and eyes. His only doubt was how soon that time would come. He sought for an answer to his riddle from the oracle of the provinces. If they would take the brilliant comedy to their hearts, washed clean of its associations by the passage of the years, it would receive what it had not yet received, its deserved recognition at the hands of the London Press and public. Before, the man had eclipsed his work. Alexander gave fourteen performances of the play, but the oracle's answer was obscure, as is the way with oracles. *The Importance of Being Earnest* did better than *The Awakening*, a failure in London, but not as well as those old warriors *The Idler* and *Liberty Hall*, or his new play

Collected and compiled by T Sturge Moore, edited by Cecil Lewis, Peter Davies, 1939 p. 112.

> *The Wilderness....* The revival was fairly successful. The comedy
> ran for fifty-five nights to average takings of £110 and, eked out
> with matinees of *Liberty Hall*, kept the balance-sheet in order.[3]

As it was, according to Barry Duncan, "Applause and no disturbance
warranted St James's presentation".[4]

The London run wasn't much of a gamble in the first place. Alexander
had intended that the year would open with Stephen Phillips's *Paolo and
Francesca*. Alexander had had difficulty casting the lead roles but had
eventually cast Henry Ainley, who had been in touring productions but
only once in the West End, as Paolo, and Evelyn Millard – the original
Cecily in the first run of *Earnest* – as Francesca.

For this production of *Earnest* the only member of the 1895 cast was
George Alexander, who reprised his role as John Worthing. Graham
Browne played Algernon, and Miss M Talbot Lady Bracknell, as they had
on tour. Bessie Page and Margaret Halstan took over the roles of Miss
Prism and Gwendolen respectively. Lilian Braithwaite was Cicely and R.E.
Goddard, Merriman. Lane was played by Herbert Dansey, of whom we
will hear more as manager of his own company in 1905.

Alexander's nervousness about how the play would be received extended
to the absence of Wilde's name on programme and publicity – "By the
author of Lady Windermere's Fan". The critic for *The Stage* noted this:

> For some apparently good reason, the name of its brilliant
> writer is left unmentioned, but yet some acknowledgment should
> be made of the fact that it came from the pen of the unhappy
> Oscar Wilde, three other of whose plays – *Lady Windermere's
> Fan*, *An Ideal Husband*, and *A Woman of No Importance* – have
> latterly been acted pretty frequently, and again with some
> success.

The reviews were generally favourable: the *Illustrated London News* damned
with faint praise by suggesting the play was a "delightful imbroglio of just
sufficiently inconsequent fooling" and "just what late diners of today require
at the theatre". *The Stage*, taking it for granted that it was a "sparkling and
even extravagantly epigrammatic farcical comedy", nevertheless compared
this production with the first night in 1895. Many in the audience would

---

3 *Sir George Alexander and the St James's Theatre*, A.E.W. Mason, Macmillan,
1935 p. 150-51.

4 *The St James's Theatre: its strange and complete history 1835-1957*, Barry
Duncan, Barrie & Rockliff, 1964 p. 262.

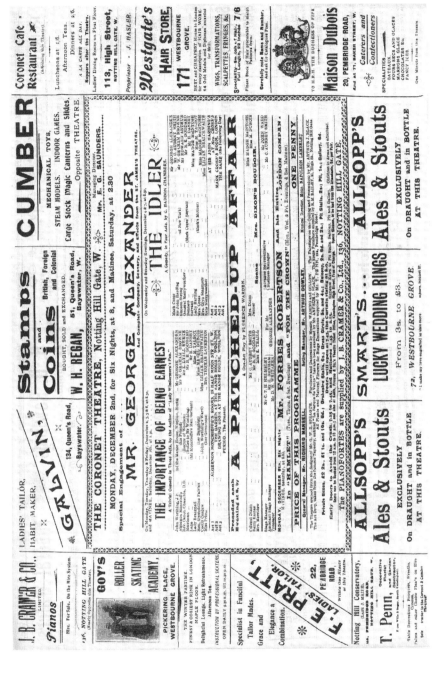

Fig. 8 *The Importance of Being Earnest*, Coronet Theatre, Notting Hill, 1901. RHC RW/11/1/5/2 RHUL Archives.

have recalled that night and although the first cast had "capable successors" they "may not perhaps make us quite forget those in whose shoes they now tread". The actresses playing the two girls gave "performances that do these rapidly advancing ladies very great credit"; Chasuble was "suave and oily-toned" and Prism was played "on quite unhackneyed lines". The two male leads played "with gaiety and spirit" and both "caused immense fun". As usual with early productions of *Earnest*, Lady Bracknell barely receives a mention, but on this occasion she was "cleverly effective".

Max Beerbohm wrote a long review in *The Saturday Review*:

> Last week, at the St James's, was revived "The Importance of Being Earnest," after an abeyance of exactly seven years – those seven years which, according to scientists, change every molecule in the human body, leaving nothing of what was there before. And yet to me the play came out fresh and exquisite as ever, and over the whole house almost every line was sending ripples of laughter – cumulative ripples that became waves, and receded only for fear of drowning the next line. In kind the play always was unlike any other, and in its kind it still seems perfect.

Max had been in America with his brother and had not attended the first night of *Earnest* in 1895; he probably didn't go until late in that first run, but he clearly remembered the play well:

> A classic must be guarded jealously. Nothing should be added to, or detracted from, a classic. In the revival at the St James's, I noted several faults of textual omission.

To a modern audience, perhaps the most important of those faults is Lady Bracknell's omission of the words, "The line is immaterial". Although this was an omission from the original script, Max was on dangerous ground as it was not at all clear whether the cast were using that original script or the augmented version published in 1899.

It wasn't just textual anomalies that attracted Max's ire. The acting was not to his taste. George Alexander and Graham Browne "rattled through their parts… Even in the second act, when not only the situation, but also the necessity for letting the audience realise the situation, demands that John Worthing should make the slowest of entries, Mr Alexander came bustling on at break-neck speed." This contrasts with his performance in 1895 where his long slow walk from the back of the stage in mourning dress was one of the highlights of the night. The other actors managed to lower the play "towards the plane of ordinary farce". As Gwendolen, Margaret Halstan acted "in the direction of burlesque" and Lyall Swete as

Chasuble "slurred" and seemed to think he was supposed to be portraying "a minutely realistic character study of a typical country clergyman".

The only exception in Max's eyes was Lilian Braithwaite, "who acted in precisely the right key of grace and dignity. She alone, in seeming to take her part quite seriously, showed that she had realised the full extent of its fun".

Max concluded with direct criticism of Alexander:

> I wish he would reconsider his theory of the play, call some rehearsals, and have his curtain rung up not at 8.5 but at 8.15. ….. I hope he is not going to have "Paolo and Francesca" rattled through. The effect on it would be quite as bad as on "The Importance of Being Earnest" – though not, I assure him, worse.

Whatever the verdict on the acting, *The Stage* reported that:

> Just as at the Coronet a month ago, *The Importance of Being Earnest* was received with acclamation and numerous curtain-calls on Tuesday …

The acclamation was such that, on 11 February, it was reported that:

> The King and Queen again evidenced their interest in the stage last night when, in company with Princess Victoria and Prince and Princess Charles of Denmark, Their Majesties witnessed "The Importance of Being Earnest" at the St James's Theatre.

Theatrical royalty had attended on the first night: Mrs Kendal was "with a large party" in one of the two private boxes, and Anthony Hope was in the other "no less amused". In the stalls were Sir Squire Bancroft and Lewis Waller.

The Stage concluded:

> Indeed, the revival made a palpable hit, and it is to be hoped that Mr Alexander will retain the play in his permanent repertory.

Alexander did not act on this suggestion, and *The Importance of Being Earnest* did not return to the professional stage in the West End until after the period covered by this book. But 1902 saw *Earnest* premiered in Germany (as *Bunbury*, at the Kleines Theater, Berlin) and revived for the first time in America. Of the production at the Empire Theatre in New York, the New York Times said:

> The play happens to be inextricably associated with the saddest and most revolting scandal in the history of the English drama, perhaps of all drama. Every man of intelligence, no doubt, wishes to disassociate the man Oscar Wilde from the playwright.[5]

---

5 Quoted in *Oscar Wilde on Stage and Screen*, Robert Tanitch, Methuen, 1999, p. 262.

Fig. 9 Fan used by Lilian Braithwaite in *Lady Windermere's Fan*, St James's Theatre, London, 1904. Private Collection.

There may not have been a professional production, but a year later the Bancroft Amateur Dramatic Club staged *Earnest* at the Regent Street Polytechnic, which in strictly geographic terms should count as the West End. The play "was given to a large audience, which taxed the capacity of the pretty little Polytechnic theatre to its utmost". "Mr Frank Harrington's orchestra was in attendance, and played several popular pieces during the evening."

As with *Earnest*, *Lady Windermere's Fan* had circled London for some time, getting closest to the centre in 1900 and 1901. This time the Bancroft Amateur Dramatic Club beat George Alexander to it, presenting *Lady Windermere's Fan* to "a crowded and fashionable audience" at St George's Hall in February 1900. Alexander took until November 1904 to make room for the play in a season at the St James's Theatre.

The Western Daily Press commented:

> To-morrow week Mr Alexander revives Oscar Wilde's wonderful play, "Lady Windermere's Fan." It is understood that the author's name will not be on the play-bills and programmes. It seems somewhat hypocritical, especially when "The Woman without a Smile" is drawing big houses. It has been suggested that there be a season of Wilde revivals; it would undoubtedly show some of our essentially modern playwrights in a very

EVERY EVENING at 9 o'clock,

Will be Acted a Play in Four Acts, entitled

LADY WINDERMERE'S FAN

By OSCAR WILDE.

Lord Windermere ...	Mr. BEN WEBSTER
Lord Darlington ...	Mr. C. AUBREY SMITH
	(By arrangement with Mr. Cyril Maude)
Lord Augustus Lorton ...	Mr. SYDNEY BROUGH
Mr. Charles Dumby ...	Mr. A. VANE-TEMPEST
	(the Original Character)
Mr. Cecil Graham ...	Mr. LESLIE FABER
Mr. Hopper ...	Mr. SELWYN SEYMOUR
Parker ...	Mr. MURRAY CARRINGTON
Lady Windermere ...	Miss LILIAN BRAITHWAITE
The Duchess of Berwick ...	Miss FANNY COLEMAN
	(the Original Character)
Lady Plimdale ...	Miss PAULINE FRENCH
Lady Cowper-Cowper ...	Miss EILEEN LEWIS
Laidy Jedburgh ...	Miss ELINOR AICKIN
Lady Agatha Carlisle ...	Miss BABARA HANNAY
Rosalie ...	Miss MAUD HARCOURT
Mrs. Erlynne ...	Miss MARION TERRY
	(the Original Character)

Act I.	...	Morning-room in Lord Windermere's House
Act II.	...	Drawing-room in Lord Windermere's House
Act III.	...	Lord Darlington's Rooms
Act IV.	...	Morning-room in Lord Windermere's House

Preceded, at 8.15, by a Play in One Act, entitled

THE DECREE NISI

By JOSHUA BATES.

Sir Adrian Hudspeth, Bart. ...	Mr. CHARLES FULTON
Dick Blundell ...	Mr. LESLIE FABER
Waiter ...	Mr. GERALD JEROME
Harper ...	Miss BABARA HANNAY
Lady Hudspeth ...	Miss MADGE McINTOSH

Scene ... Lady Hudspeth's Private Sitting-room at the Marlborough Hotel, London.

Time—The Present.

LUNCH, 2/6. DINNER, 7/6.
ONE MINUTE'S WALK FROM THIS THEATRE.
Greatly renowned for excellent Cuisine. Elegant Suite of Rooms for Private Dinners and Banquets.
The Celebrated THEATRE DINNER, 5/6, the very best in London (à la Carte). Popular Prices.
NO SUPPERS.

RESTAURANT DIEUDONNÉ
RYDER STREET, ST. JAMES'S STREET.

Programme of Music.

OVERTURE ...	"Stradella" ...	Flotow
SELECTION ...	"La Poupée" ...	Audran
SERENADE ...	"Hongroise" ...	V. Joncieres
RIGADOON ...		Clamende
CZARAS ...		Michiels
MINUET ...		Fanaloi
VALSE ...		Berger
SELECTION ...	"Messenger Boy" ...	Caryll-Monckton

The Scenery Painted by Mr. WALTER HANN.

Mesdames Braithwaite, French, Lewis and Hamilton's Gowns by Madame Fannian, Lower Grosvenor Place; Miss Terry's by Madame Hayward, New Bond Street; Miss Coleman's by Marshall and Snelgrove; the others by Madame Brown, Knightsbridge, and Mrs. Evans. Hats by Madame Elain, New Bond Street. Wigs by W. Clarkson, and C. H. Fox.

The Furniture by Wiseman & Butcher, Ltd., 7, High Street, Kennington, and Ernest Renton, King Street, St. James's, S.W.

Machinist, J. Cullen. Electrician, W. Babioce. Property Master, H. S. Henry.

INTERVALS—Ten Minutes after each Act.

MATINEES OF BOTH PLAYS EVERY WEDNESDAY and SATURDAY at 2.15.

The Proof Engravings and Etchings in the Vestibule and on the Staircase are supplied by Messrs. Dowdeswell, 160, New Bond Street, W.

NO FEES. No Charge for Programmes or Cloak Room Attendants. NO FEES.

The Attendants are strictly forbidden to accept gratuities, and are liable to instant dismissal should they do so. Visitors to the Theatre are earnestly begged to assist the Management in carrying out a regulation framed for their comfort and convenience.

Doors open at 8. Commence at 8.15. Carriages at 11.

PRICES.—Private Boxes, £4 4s. Stalls, 10s. 6d. Dress Circle, 7s. 6d. Upper Boxes, Numbered and Reserved, Front Row, 5s.; Other Rows, 4s. Pit, 2s. 6d. Gallery, 1s. Box Office (Mr. E. Arnold) Open 10 till 10. Seats can be booked by Letter, Telegram ("Parthenia, London") or Telephone (No. 3902 Gerrard).

The Scenery in this Theatre has been rendered fireproof by the NON-FLAMABLE WOOD FABRICS Co., Ltd.

SUNDAY { LUNCHEONS / DINNERS } A FEATURE.
Telegrams—"Suffoat, London."

Fig. 10 *Lady Windermere's Fan*, St. James's Theatre, London, 1904. Private Collection.

bad light. The remarkable thing about Wilde's wit was that the superficial ring of it hid from the thoughtless a depth of philosophy. A complete edition of Wilde's works would be even more welcome than a series of revivals.

The press advertisements for the play did carry Wilde's name, as did the playbills and the programme.

The play opened on Saturday 19 November; the press were undecided as to whether it had been ten or twelve years since the first production but there was no doubt that there was "a brilliant audience," and that it "caused great delight to theatregoers". Some of the atmosphere was caught by Charles Ricketts in his journal entry for that day:

> The first night of the revival of *Lady Windermere's Fan*. Who should sit next to us but Ross; the biographer of Oscar Wilde in the *Encyclopaedia Britannica* sat in front; the house was full of friends and enemies.[6]

Ross and Ricketts reminisced and talked about Wilde's time in gaol. A few days later Ricketts recorded reading an early copy of *De Profundis*. But he was ambivalent about the play:

> The play was poorly acted, without spirit or refinement. The first act has worn well, the second and third less well, the wit is as new as ever. I feared it might have aged. It is in the dramatic business, the soliloquies and a touch or two of rhetoric, that the thing has aged.[7]

Still, "the audience was enthusiastic".

Max Beerbohm again reviewed for the *Saturday Review*, but in a long and thoughtful piece which contrasts the work of Oscar Wilde with that of Maurice Maeterlinck, only one paragraph is given to the performance itself. "The present performance at the St James's is not very good on the lighter side – the more important side. Some of the characters, in coping with the witticisms, subside into tragic earnestness, others into roystering farce." Aubrey Smith, as Lord Darlington comes in for especial criticism for saying the 'extravagant silly things' for which Lady Windermere tells him off, "as though his life and hers depended on them", and delivering a line "with all the portentousness of an eminent physician examining an invalid". Marion Terry, who remained from the original cast as Mrs Erlynne, "still has no rival in what may be called the graciousness of

6 Ricketts, p. 112.

7 Ibid.

Fig. 11 *Lady Windermere's Fan*, Act III, St. James's Theatre, London, 1904. Private Collection.

91

pathos," and Lilian Braithwaite is again singled out for praise from a generally lacklustre cast.

Marion Terry received universally good reviews, the *Daily Telegraph* declaring that she "swept the whole house along with her by a performance as powerful, as convincing, as accomplished as anything this admirable artist has ever done". The *Sheffield Daily Telegraph* thought highly of Miss Terry but was less certain about the play:

> Should there be any who like to renew acquaintance with what was known as the "fin de siècle" drama, they can do so in "Lady Windermere's Fan" at the St James's, where it has been staged by Mr George Alexander as a stop-gap until he discovers some more romantic successor. Amongst the actors and actresses are Mr Aubrey Smith, the cricketer, Mr Ben Webster, Miss Marion Terry (who is doing marvellous things in her old part), and Miss Lilian Braithwaite, one of the sweetest players on the London stage.

Others were disconcerted that George Alexander was not taking part in the play, although he had explained this as preparing for a new experiment in performing in new plays at matinees later in the season. One reviewer thought that his presence in the audience on the opening night made the cast nervous, with Ben Webster "held in a kind of rigidity from this cause". The *Yorkshire Post* thought Marion Terry was "to the front too little nowadays" and wondered "why her gifts are so sparingly used". Echoing Ricketts's thoughts, The *Sheffield Daily Telegraph* summed up:

> The artifice of the whole, indeed, stands out with quite an old-fashioned touch in the prevalent soliloquies and asides. However, West End playgoers have in recent years seen nothing of a work with which provincial audiences have been made familiar by many reproductions, and the amazing cleverness of the unhappy author in what was his first play came with a good deal of the force of a new work. The reception, at all events, was enthusiastic.

A Woman of No Importance had toured more extensively than any of the other three plays during this period, and had, like the others although not quite as often, come close to the West End. It was not until 1907, however, that this perennial favourite of provincial audiences was finally given a West End revival.

On his return from what appears to have been a successful visit with his company to Berlin, Beerbohm Tree announced that he would be staging a revival of *A Woman of No Importance* at His Majesty's Theatre from 22 May.

By this time there was no problem about admitting who had written the play and it was advertised as by Oscar Wilde. Again, it received a warm welcome; the *Manchester Courier* said:

> It is just over fourteen years since Mr Tree produced "A Woman of No Importance" at the Haymarket Theatre. Yet the play wears wonderfully well, and it had an enthusiastic welcome on its revival at His Majesty's Theatre to-night. That warm welcome was well-deserved, for the piece is good drama in every sense, and, apart from the poignant story, its cleverness of characterisation and the brilliance of its dialogue, puts to shame much of the pretentious theatrical work of to-day.

The actors were "called again and again at the close of each act". Unusually, the set came in for praise of its own:

> As a piece of this description is too small – in a theatrical sense – for so spacious a stage as that of His Majesty's, Mr Tree has erected an elaborate gilt frame behind the proscenium and thus obtains the effect of a comparatively small stage. It is a capital idea and one that is wonderfully effective.

Marion Terry, as Mrs Arbuthnot had "never acted more exquisitely" and "added another laurel to her crown". Of Tree's performance as Lord Illingworth, it was admitted that "Much water has passed under London Bridge since he first essayed the role, but time seems to make little difference to Mr Tree" and as well as being "excellent", he spoke the "brilliant phrases put into his mouth as if they were naturally delivered." From most reviewers the whole cast for once won equal praise; but there were dissenters. *The Illustrated London News* thought that

> Marion Terry never strikes a deep enough note of distress in the earlier acts nor displays enough contempt in the closing scene.

The Times trumpeted its modernity by saying that nowadays "people don't talk in plays as Oscar Wilde made them talk…. The truth is a little of it goes a long way and in *A Woman of No Importance* there is far too much of it."

Perhaps a little did go a long way for Edwardian audiences. The play lasted for only 45 performances and closed on 5 July.

6. 1901 – 1908 AND THE RITZ

Charles Ricketts records in his journal for 23 September 1905:

> In the evening to see revival of the Ideal Husband at the
> Coronet, done by a provincial company. I was surprised to find
> it much better than I had thought. I remember Oscar saying
> of it, when he insisted on our being present at the first night:
> "It was written for ridiculous puppets to play, and the critics
> will say, "Ah, here is Oscar unlike himself!" – though in reality
> I became engrossed in writing it, and it contains a great deal of
> the real Oscar." This is a formal and a severe estimate of it. Oscar
> was always better than he thought he was, and no one in his life
> time was able to see it, including my clairvoyant self.[1]

We have seen that George Alexander revived *The Importance of Being
Earnest* at the St James's Theatre in 1902. He toured that production on a
restricted circuit in the last months of 1901, going to Manchester, Belfast,
Dublin, Nottingham and Glasgow as well as the suburbs of London. The
cast for the tour was slightly different from the one that appeared at the
St James's, one notable change being the part of Lane. On tour Algernon's
servant was played by J Lennox Pawle, who had trained at Sarah Thorne's
Dramatic School in Margate. He appeared in the East End as a comedian
before coming into the West End in 1892 and appearing in a number of
"controversial" plays. One of these – *Tommy Atkins* at the Duke of York's
Theatre – called forth from William Archer

> an outrageous East-end melodrama beside which the ordinary
> Adelphi drama seems a work of high literary distinction. I
> sat out two preposterous acts, not unamusing in their very
> extravagance, and then could endure no more.[2]

Later he joined Frank Benson's touring company, but Pawle's main

---

1 Quoted in *Self-Portrait, taken from the Letters and Journals of Charles Ricketts,
R A*. Collected and compiled by T Sturge Moore. Edited by Cecil Lewis. Peter
Davies 1939, p. 124. Ricketts may have been mistaken about the date. 23
September was a Saturday; an announcement earlier in the month had said
that the tour would start on Monday 25 September – a more usual day of the
week to start a run. That announcement also said that Miss Henrietta Watson
would play the principal female part but she does not appear to have been in
the company at all.

2 *The Theatrical 'World' of 1896*, William Archer. Walter Scott, 1897, p. 9.

interest here is that he was a friend of Wilde's, being very close to Ernest Dowson, and mixing in a crowd with Beardsley and others. His particular friend was Marmaduke Langdale, who has been mentioned in an earlier chapter.

In 1904, William Archer and Harley Granville Barker produced a detailed scheme for a National Theatre. They did not feel able to publish in more than a privately printed, very limited edition at the time but issued it to the general public in 1907. The detailed scheme did not change between those dates. One of the very detailed chapters dealt with the proposed repertory and showed nine "modern English plays" being revived – that is plays first performed after 1870. Among these nine is *The Importance of Being Earnest*. Archer and Barker explained their choices thus

> Though, in selecting modern plays for revival, we have in the main deferred to the generally expressed theatrical taste of the past ten or twelve years, we do not wish to imply an opinion that this taste is all that can be desired, or that it would be specially fostered by the National Theatre. On the contrary, we believe that the "society play" – the drama of "frocks and frills" – bulks far too largely on the stage of to-day; and one of the chief advantages of the National Theatre would lie in its providing an escape from the conditions which at present are thought to impose this type of play upon both managers and authors. There is no doubt that a large section of the public is being gradually alienated from the theatre by a sense of the monotony of the fare provided; and as we were bound to choose from among existing plays, we could not help, in some measure, reproducing that monotony.[3]

The early months of 1901 saw the winding down of tours that had started earlier: Beatrice Homer's *A Woman of No Importance*, and T B Thalberg's *Lady Windermere's Fan*. But most of the year – from May to November – was taken up by a single touring company under the management of Cecil Klein and Fred Ash. They paired *Lady Windermere's Fan* and *The Importance of Being Earnest*, splitting each week between the two plays. Klein was an American born actor and although he had toured the provinces, this was the first time he had taken his own company. It may be that, although he managed to get bookings, he was inexperienced in publicity for he seems to have been infrequently reviewed or advertised. An example of one of the few mentions in local papers is headed "Amusements at Bexhill":

---

3 *A National Theatre*, William Archer and H Granville Barker, Duckworth 1907, p. 42 et seq.

The weather at Bexhill-on-Sea during the past week has been magnificent. The De La Warr Orchestra plays in the Kursaal every day and Cecil Klein and Fred Ash's Company have been acting "Lady Windermere's Fan" and "The Importance of Being Earnest" during the week. The hunting season promises well. So successful was the first Bexhill subscription ball that a second will take place at the Metropole on Friday, November 29. A semi-official banquet has been decided upon which will take place at one of the hotels on the day following the ball, and a distinguished company is expected to attend.

Oddly, this comes from a local newspaper in Manchester, over two hundred miles from Bexhill. A more local paper described "a very capable company of artistes". *Lady Windermere's Fan* was said to be "the well-known society drama," but *The Importance of Being Earnest* had to have the description "(a farcical comedy)" added.

When they appeared at St Anne's on the Sea, there was competition

The town is quite full, and the accommodation is greatly taxed. A special band is playing three times a day on the Esplanade, and will do so till September, and good companies are appearing at the Public Hall Theatre. This week "Lady Windermere's Fan" is being presented. Golfers are present in force, and the four clubs in the district have their links in full use.

This is reminiscent of Cicely's "the weather continues charming" in *Earnest*.

On 21 November *The Stage* reported that Klein and Ash had "recently concluded a successful fourteen weeks tour of 'Lady Windermere's Fan' and 'The Importance of Being Earnest'". Early November may have been a natural point at which to end the tour, but it was forced by George Alexander taking the decision to tour his own company in *The Importance of Being Earnest* prior to its West End revival.

At about the same time as the announcement in *The Stage*, Cecil Klein was already appearing in *The Red Lamp* by Outram Tristram at the Theatre Royal, Leamington. Klein and Ash had secured the touring rights to this from Beerbohm Tree.

Alexander's tour began in Liverpool and then travelled to Manchester, where the local press were confused; one paper said the play "was given here a few weeks ago," while another claimed it had "not previously been seen on the Manchester stage. Alexander repeated his performance as John Worthing, but there were no other members of the original cast. Algy was played by W Graham Browne, then married to the actress Madge McIntosh and later to Marie Tempest. Browne had worked with Tree at the Haymarket and toured with Benson as well as acting as a producer. Apart from these two, perhaps the best known names to provincial audiences at the time were E Lyall Swete (who had also toured with Benson) as Canon Chasuble and Lennox Pawle.

Reflecting the relative unimportance of the role of Lady Bracknell in early productions of *Earnest*, she was played on tour and when the play reached the St James's by Miss M Talbot. Miss Talbot had been little more than an extra in the St James's company for a while, although it is not clear which of the three Miss M Talbots then acting – M, Marjory or Mildred – this one might have been. Cicely was played by Lilian Braithwaite – again, not well known, although she was to become a favourite on the West-End stage and, much later in her career, to take the female lead in Noel Coward's *The Vortex*.

The adverts for the tour still showed *Earnest* as "by the Author of 'Lady Windermere's Fan'" but the repertoire for the tour also included *The Wilderness, Liberty Hall* and *The Awakening*, and their authors – H V Esmond, C Haddon Chambers and R C Carton respectively – were credited. *Earnest* was followed at ten o'clock each evening by the one act *A Patched-Up Affair* by Florence Warden, which featured W Graham Browne's wife Madge McIntosh. In Manchester the press greeted the play as "the late Oscar Wilde's clever comedy," and a "brilliant comedy". The local press appeared to like the idea of putting the supporting one act play on after the main feature. It

> should as a general thing – when one act plays are needed to eke out the shortness of the main dish of the evening – prove very popular with playgoers. The latter can then get away comfortably at ten o'clock to catch their trains, besides being spared the infliction of sitting through an invertebrate and often silly concoction which serves no other purpose than that of a make weight. In the present instance it so happens that the short piece "A Patched-up Affair," is thoroughly worth seeing, but the vast majority of what we call curtain raisers only raise sighs and yawns and wonderment that they should be performed at all.

One local critic threw up his hands:

> So far as the poor, long-suffering critic is concerned, the critic who likes to discover a definite form and trend in what he criticises, he is necessarily at sea until he abandons so ridiculous an attitude as that which demands consistency, and merely settles down to be indiscriminately amused.

Another dealt with it on a purely practical level:

> The fog did not prevent a large audience gathering at the Theatre Royal last night, nor did it dim the glitter of a very clever play.

Lyall Swete was "excellent" as Chasuble, Alexander gave "a finished reading" as Worthing, W Graham Browne was "a capital Algernon Moncrieffe" and Lilian Braithwaite gave "a good performance" as Cicely. The other roles, including Lady Bracknell are lumped together as being "well acted" or not mentioned at all.

After Oxford, Belfast, Dublin and Nottingham the interest in the play became greater as it moved closer to London and *The Stage* went overboard when it opened at the Coronet Theatre in Notting Hill. This was the first week in December and the Coronet was advertising itself as "The premier Theatre on the Central London Railway, and most accessible Theatre during the Foggy Weather".

Despite the Manchester critic's appreciation of the post play one-acter, at the Coronet, *A Patched-up Affair* was played as a curtain raiser. Rather than play the full repertory of plays as he had done in Manchester and elsewhere, here only *Earnest* and *The Idler* were played, with *Earnest* being performed on Monday, Tuesday, Thursday and Friday evenings and the Saturday matinee. *The Idler* only managed Wednesday and Saturday evenings.

The opening lines of the review in *The Stage* read:

> Never before, perhaps, in the history of the Notting Hill playhouse has such genuine enthusiasm prevailed at any presentment as that which attended Mr George Alexander's revival of The Importance of Being Earnest on Monday evening. The instantaneous success of this brilliantly written farcical piece, the spontaneity of the laughter and applause of a crowded audience – far from exclusively local – should encourage Mr Alexander to stage it once again on his return to the St James's

The actors were all praised but, "taking the play in a brisk and lively time throughout, were evidently unprepared for the extraordinary hilarity of the audience". There were two or three curtain calls at the end of the first and second acts and five at the end of the play, with Alexander having to appear finally alone to take the applause. The reviewer then felt the need to recapitulate the entire plot over many column inches.

The early months of 1902 saw little Wilde: Nina Cressy's tour of *An Ideal Husband* visited Drogheda and Brighton and there was the first notice of an amateur production of that play, at the Royal County Theatre in Reading. There were also six nights of *Earnest* at the Crystal Palace Theatre. This was put on by the Frank Weathersby Company which does not appear in connection with Wilde again in this period. The programme credits Oscar Wilde and lists his other plays, including one called *Lady Wiedernerer's Lane*. The programme is full of errors, including a servant called Dane Lane, a "Cecily Carcrew" and the removal of Jack's home from Hertfordshire to Herefordshire. For the convenience of patrons the programme prints the railway timetable and assures them that "this theatre is disinfected with Jeyes' Fluid." Weathersby had begun as a sixteen year old actor in pantomime and had toured overseas extensively as both actor and manager. Shortly after this outing with *Earnest* he settled down as a theatrical agent.

In 1902, Arthur Hare enjoyed a successful tour of *A Pair of Spectacles*, and *A Fool's Paradise*, travelling to "all the better number-two towns". Then, according to Ben Iden Payne

> Arthur Hare decided to make what was regarded at the time as a bold move. He determined to tour *The Importance of Being Earnest*. Since the scandal of Oscar Wilde's trial and imprisonment, no one had ventured to give performances of his plays. Hare persuaded the copyright owners to let him do so without announcing the author's name, which would still have been unthinkable. So all the billing and the programs stated that the play was "A comedy by the author of *A Woman of No Importance*." The device worked.[4]

Payne is clearly wrong here, although Hare may have sold the production to his company on this basis. The tour, according to Payne, opened at the New Theatre, Oxford:

> This choice of theatre turned out to be more right than we knew. Besides again acting as stage manager, I played Canon Chasuble. On the opening night I happened to be in the property room shortly before my first entrance. A row of black-bound books on a shelf inspired me with the notion that it might be appropriate for the canon to be seen holding what looked like an open Bible. My entrance was imminent, so as I pulled out one of the books I had time only to notice that they were the annual registers of the students resident at Oxford University.

---

4 *A Life in a Wooden O: Memoirs of the Theatre* by Ben Iden Payne, Yale University Press 1977, p. 45.

CRYSTAL PALACE THEATRE.

Business Manager   -   -   -   J. E. SHARPE.
Musical Director   -   -   -   LEONARD GAUTIER.

PROGRAMME.

MONDAY, MARCH 31st for SIX NIGHTS at 7.45.
Matinee, Wednesday, at 3.

Mr. FRANK WEATHERSBY'S COMPANY
By Arrangement with Sir George Alexander.

THE IMPORTANCE OF BEING EARNEST.

A Trivial Comedy for Serious People by OSCAR WILDE.

Author of "A Woman of No Importance," "An Ideal Husband," "Salome," "Lady Wiedermerer Lane."

THE PHENOMENAL SUCCESS AT THE ST. JAMES' THEATRE, W.

CAST :

John Worthing, J.P. (of the Manor House Woolton, Herefordshire)	Mr. HAROLD WESTON
Algernon Moncrieff (his friend)	Mr. JULIAN D'ALBIE
Rev. Canon Chasuible, D.D. (Rector of Woolton)	Mr. EDWIN MERVYN
Merriman (Butler to Mr. Worthing)	Mr. ERIC H. ALBURY
Dane Lane (Man Servant to Mr. Moncrieff)...	Mr. HAROLD BARISTON
Lady Bracknell..	Miss MAUD KIRWAN
Hon. Gwendoline Fairfax (her Daughter) ...	Miss MAY SAKER
Cecily Carcrew (John Worthing's Ward) ...	Miss MARGARET BOYD
Miss Prism	Miss DOT SEILBY

Act 1   ...   Algernon Moncrieff's Rooms in Half-Moon St., W.
Act 2   ...   ...   The Garden at the Manor House, Woolton
Act 3   ...   ...   Morning Room at the Manor House, Woolton

The Play produced by Mr. Gerald Ames. —Direct from the St. James', W.

General Manager   -   Mr. EDWARD MERVYN.

PROGRAMME OF MUSIC.

Overture   .... "La Dame Blanche" .... *Boieldieu*
Selection .... "The Yeomen of the Guard" .... *Arthur Sullivan*
Piccolo Solo   .... "Tarantella" .... *W. H. Rimmer*
Mr. H. CRAFTS.
Characteristique Orientale   .... "Kismet" .... *J. D. Markey*
March .... "Under the Double Eagle" .... *J. F. Wagner*
GOD SAVE THE KING.
The Orchestra under the direction of Mr. LEONARD GAUTIER.

MONDAY, APRIL 14th for 6 Nights and Wednesday Matinee,

BELLA DONNA from the St. James' Theatre.

Fig. 12 *The Importance of Being Earnest*, Crystal Palace Theatre, London, 1902. Private Collection.

101

As I reached the center of the stage I opened the volume and, looking down, saw the words "Oscar Fingal O'Flahertie Wills Wilde." The coincidence so startled me that I almost forgot the words of my entering speech.[5]

No record of a performance in Oxford has been found and it seems to have been a sporadic tour. In July and August the company visited Great Yarmouth, Scarborough and Gloucester. This last, on Monday 4 August, marked the day on which the local theatres re-opened "after the summer vacation". Similarly, the booking in Great Yarmouth in July was for the theatre's opening week and Hare began with *A Pair of Spectacles*, later in the week *A Fool's Paradise* with *Earnest* opening on the Friday. It was clear that *Earnest* was not the focus of the tour, being played only on Friday, while *A Pair of Spectacles* played for four of the six nights; in Gloucester *Earnest* only played on Wednesday. This meant that the reviewers concentrated on that play and only mentioned *Earnest* as a coming attraction.

Hare's newspaper adverts did not even go as far as Payne had suggested; they did not indicate an author for *Earnest* at all, but nor did they for any other play in the repertory. The local paper in Great Yarmouth referred to "the enormously successful farcical comedy ... by the author of Lady Windermere's Fan, A Woman of No Importance, &c." Each of the plays had as a curtain raiser, a "new musical one-act play" by Richard Temple called *Two to One* featuring "the well-known baritone" Mr William Chatham, Miss Kate S Beck, contralto and Miss Le Page.

Following these three dates Hare seems to have interrupted the tour, starting again for another three dates in May and June 1903. In the meantime he had been touring a revival of Robert Buchanan's play *A Man's Shadow*, which had played in March and April in Bedford, Lincoln and Leeds. After the three *Earnests* he appears to have continued touring *A Pair of Spectacles*, but without *Earnest* in the repertory.

After just over a year's absence, *A Woman of No Importance* started touring again in August 1902. The company was variously billed as Mr J Y F Cooke's and Miss Madge McIntosh and Mr Charles V France's. McIntosh, who had recently been touring with Alexander, played Mrs Arbuthnot and France Lord Illingworth. The play was a lesser attraction than Henry Arthur Jones's *The Case of Rebellious Susan*, which opened the week. In Great Yarmouth the local paper seemed concerned that it might not be a sufficient draw:

---

5 Idem p. 46.

It is to be trusted that the support accorded will be on a liberal scale in all parts of the house, for – particularly in the case of *A Woman of No Importance* – the productions will be found as enthralling to a gallery as to a circle audience.

Oddly, while not mentioning the author's name, the writer then said

A propos, we note Mr H J Wilde's name as business manager.

This was clearly a speculative tour; it only began in August and an advert appeared on 18 September seeking bookings for October – "to follow Scarborough", which was in the week of 22 September. The dates were filled with an appearance at Bridlington, followed by Limerick and Cork. While in Cork they advertised "offers invited for Spring", but none can have been forthcoming. The tour lasted until the end of the year but, as with the Hare tour, the Wilde play was performed late in the week and did not attract reviews. Had Wilde still been alive, surely playing second fiddle to Henry Arthur Jones would have been a worse insult than the removal of his name.

The beginning of 1903 was marked by a number of amateur productions, the first of which redefines "amateur". This was two performances of *The Importance of Being Earnest* at the Imperial Theatre, Westminster in aid of the Parochial Schools of Upper Chelsea and St Hugh's Home for Boys, Clapham. Wilde's name was printed on the front of the programme and the publishers Wright and Jones had taken the back of the programme to advertise that the works of Oscar Wilde could be bought from their premises in Ormond Row, Chelsea. Private boxes could be had for four guineas, with stalls at 10/6. Gwendolen was played by Margaret Evans-Gordon, a great-granddaughter of the actor John Kemble and mother of the actress Pamela Stanley; Miss Prism was played by the Hon. Ethel Cadogan, scion of the family which had built much of Chelsea and Knightsbridge and sometime Woman of the Bedchamber to Queen Victoria; Jack was the Hon Stephen Powys, later the 6th Baron Lilford; Chasuble was played by Arthur Hare, who we have already met touring *Earnest*; and Algernon was played by Ernest Thesiger, six years before his professional stage debut and thirteen before his first film. A thirty six piece amateur orchestra under the baton of Mr B Neville Flux provided the musical accompaniment.

The Alexander Dramatic Club performed *Lady Windermere's Fan* at the Surrey Masonic Hall in Camberwell, where "the curtain raiser was capitally rushed through," and the Athenaeum Theatre in Manchester saw a performance of *The Importance of Being Earnest* by the Lewis Waller Amateur Dramatic Club, during which "the programme was interspersed

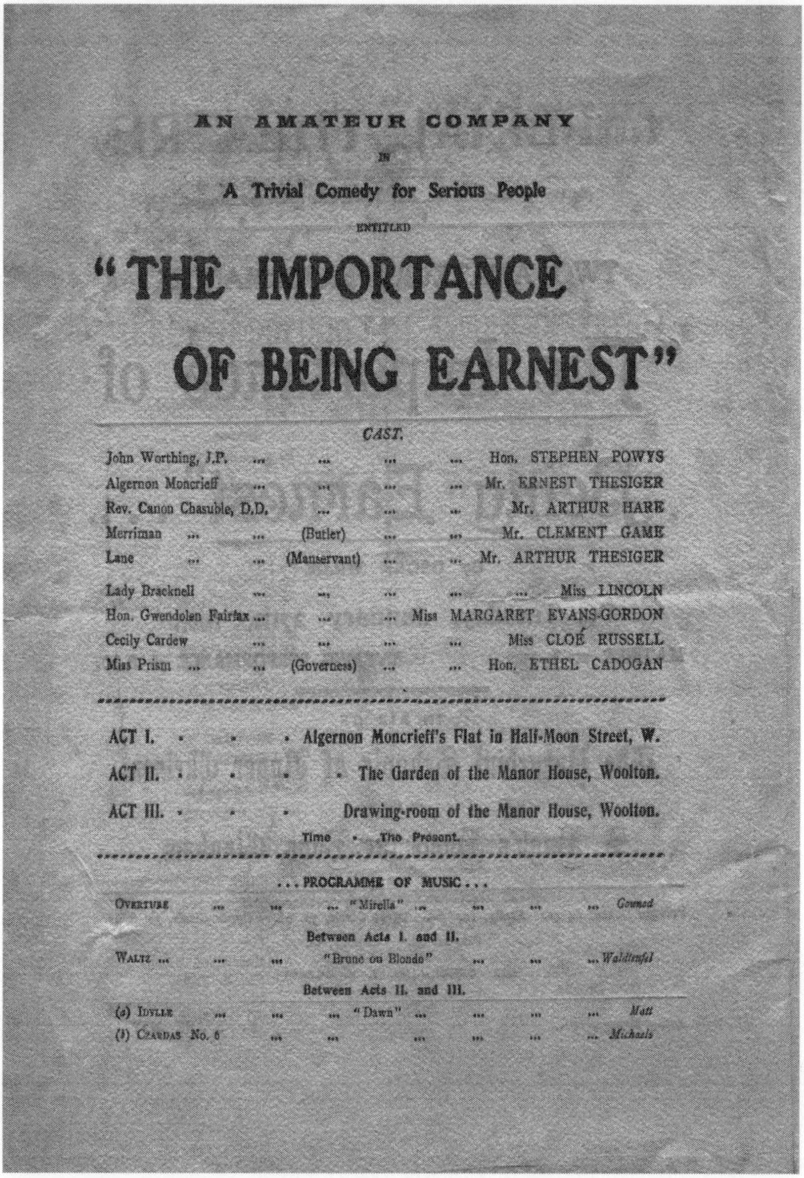

AN AMATEUR COMPANY

IN

A Trivial Comedy for Serious People

ENTITLED

"THE IMPORTANCE OF BEING EARNEST"

CAST.

John Worthing, J.P.		Hon. STEPHEN POWYS
Algernon Moncrieff		Mr. ERNEST THESIGER
Rev. Canon Chasuble, D.D.		Mr. ARTHUR HARE
Merriman	(Butler)	Mr. CLEMENT GAME
Lane	(Manservant)	Mr. ARTHUR THESIGER
Lady Bracknell		Miss LINCOLN
Hon. Gwendolen Fairfax		Miss MARGARET EVANS-GORDON
Cecily Cardew		Miss CLOÉ RUSSELL
Miss Prism	(Governess)	Hon. ETHEL CADOGAN

ACT I. - - - Algernon Moncrieff's Flat in Half-Moon Street, W.

ACT II. - - - - The Garden of the Manor House, Woolton.

ACT III. - - - Drawing-room of the Manor House, Woolton.

Time - The Present.

...PROGRAMME OF MUSIC...

OVERTURE	"Mirella"	*Gounod*

Between Acts I. and II.

WALTZ	"Brune ou Blonde"	*Waldteufel*

Between Acts II. and III.

(a) IDYLLE	"Dawn"	*Matt*
(b) CZARDAS No. 6		*Michaels*

Fig. 13 *The Importance of Being Earnest,* Imperial Theatre, London, 1903. RHC RW/11/1/5/4 RHUL Archives.

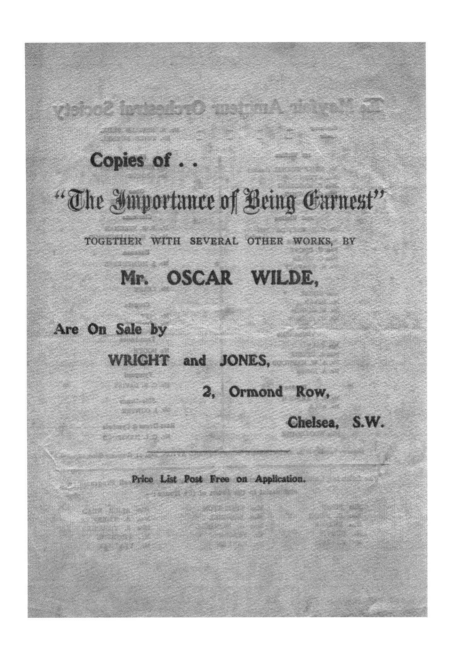

Fig. 14 "Wright & Jones" advertisement for works by Oscar Wilde, Imperial Theatre programme, 1903. RHC RW/11/1/5/4 RHUL Archives.

with selections of music by the Chorlton-cum-Hardy Orchestral Society". Two months apart, at the theatre in the Regent Street Polytechnic in London, the Bancroft Amateur Club staged *An Ideal Husband* and *The Importance of Being Earnest*, which garnered longer reviews than many professional productions.

Through the summer of 1903 the only productions were the three Arthur Hare *Earnests* and two *Earnests* by the May Pardoe company in Torquay and Teddington, about which little is known.

In August there was a production of *A Woman of No Importance* at the Crystal Palace by the Kendal Chalmers company with Charles Hartley as Lord Illingworth and Lillian Williams as Mrs Arbuthnot. This was the first stop in a substantial tour, which from here on travelled as the Charles Hartley company. At Crystal Palace the theatre had to compete against "Mr Wood's Cinematograph exhibition of the contest for the America Cup," and in the Egyptian Court "a new invention, the waltzing tops, six in number, and each capable of seating six persons." As it was a holiday weekend there was also a firework display with "a number of entertaining novelties … embracing mechanical horizontal bar performers, dismembered skeletons, and a pair of foot-balancers, besides the usual huge set-piece representing "The Road to the Derby."

Hartley's tour started with *A Woman of No Importance*, but part way through added *Lady Windermere's Fan*. Usually they performed only one play in a town but occasionally – in Brighton, Blackpool, Boscombe and Hull – they performed both. Also in the repertory were *The Idler* and *Captain Swift*. *The Idler* usually began the week and was the play which garnered the reviews. On the basis of its reception the company seems to have been well regarded.

The most interesting tour of the period was that undertaken by the Marquis of Anglesey with his own company.[6] Henry Cyril Paget, 5th Marquis of Anglesey, was an extraordinary man who had an extraordinary, but short, life. He was the son of the Earl of Uxbridge – later the 4th Marquis of Anglesey – but it was rumoured that his real father was the French actor Benoît-Constant Coquelin and it was with him that Henry lived following the death of his mother when he was two years old. When

---

6 Much of the information about the Marquis of Anglesey comes from conversations with Viv Gardner (Emerita Professor of Theatre Studies, University of Manchester) and her article "Would you trust this man with your fortune?", *Guardian*, 10 October 2007.

the 4th Marquis married again, when Henry was eight, he was taken to live in North Wales. Here he appears to have lived a lonely, and sickly, childhood but one in which he learned to speak fluent French and passable Russian and Welsh. He travelled to Germany, where he learned painting and singing. In 1898 he succeeded to the title and inherited property on Anglesey and in Staffordshire, Dorset and Derbyshire as well as an income of £110,000 a year. It took him six years to go through all that and more, bankrupting the estate.

One of his extravagances was to convert the family chapel into a theatre. This was initially a home for amateur productions for local audiences, but rapidly became a destination for touring companies. In 1901 the Marquis saw a professional company in Llandudno and, by the simple act of paying them more than they had seen before, hijacked the company's star players. He started touring with them in a number of plays and, in November 1903, started a tour of *An Ideal Husband* at St James's Hall, Lichfield. The Marquis played Lord Goring, a role which a member of the company thought could have been written for him. *The Stage* said of him that he

> acted creditably, being at his best when he circumvents the adventuress, Mrs Cheveley, brilliantly played by Miss Florence Hamer.

"The scenery and dresses were beautiful; the jewellery worn by the Marquis was very conspicuous." Jewellery and costumes were high among the Marquis's spending priorities, conspicuous consumption being what came to define him. He had his car converted so that the exhaust sprayed perfume; in London he was often seen with a poodle bedecked with pink ribbons under his arm. All his costumes were made to order – one, for a part in Aladdin, was encrusted with jewels, was reported to be worth £100,000 and his changes of costume came so often during a performance that he needed an army of dressers.

The Marquis's company at its height consisted of some fifty people and needed five trucks for the baggage and scenery. He had the scenery specially painted and many of the props were copies of furniture at Anglesey Castle. As well as actors, he took his own orchestra with him rather than hiring locally as most companies at the time would do. The Marquis travelled with a personal staff of four in a Pullman motor car. An American newspaper reported that it was well known that once a dealer had been able to get the Marquis to look at "a rare gem, the sale is practically made."

The Burton Chronicle, most unusually for a review of any provincial production mentioned not only the musical director for the production, but the stage manager, assistant stage manager and the electrician.

The following week the company was in Boscombe, at The Grand where again the reviews said the Marquis was "well suited" to the part of Lord Goring. However, a paper called *The World's News* in Australia, where the Marquis held a special fascination, gave what was perhaps a more honest view of the Boscombe appearance

> No travelling circus has ever created a greater sensation in Bournemouth's quiet suburb than the arrival on the previous Sunday of the Marquis, whose lithographed portrait adorns the window of nearly every shop in the neighbourhood.

> The only serious mishap was an accident to the specially painted scenery, which was left out in the rain by a railway official. Immediately on hearing of the accident, the Marquis, who wore a long lavender coat, tucked Fido under his arm and motored to the theatre, where he waved a white-gloved hand. This was a signal for Mr Keith, his manager, to be up and doing ....

> When the curtain rose there was only a handful of people in the large auditorium, and in the vast gallery six persons huddled together for company.

On 7 December the company came to Folkestone; he may not have had a lot of choice, not being a first or second theatre circuit troupe, but the Pleasure Gardens Folkestone in December doesn't sound like a money spinner, even though he was "living the part of Lord Goring". *The Burton Chronicle* reported that:

> The Marquis arrived by special train, made up of three first-class coaches, three large covered carriage trucks, containing personal luggage, and two large pantechnicon vans with his magnificent scenery. His Lordship's retinue comprises about 50 persons, including valets and attendants, who carefully guard the valuables.

The Folkestone Chronicle reported

> It has brought him crowded houses nearly every evening this week. As Lord Goring in "An Ideal Husband" the noble Marquis gives a fair representation of a young nobleman who is not such a fool as he appears to be. But the Marquis does not quite fill the part with that silent force and set purpose it required. Some of his lines were uttered without full significance. Lord Goring is a philosopher not a superficial monger of platitudes. He has heart and soul, discretion and courage.

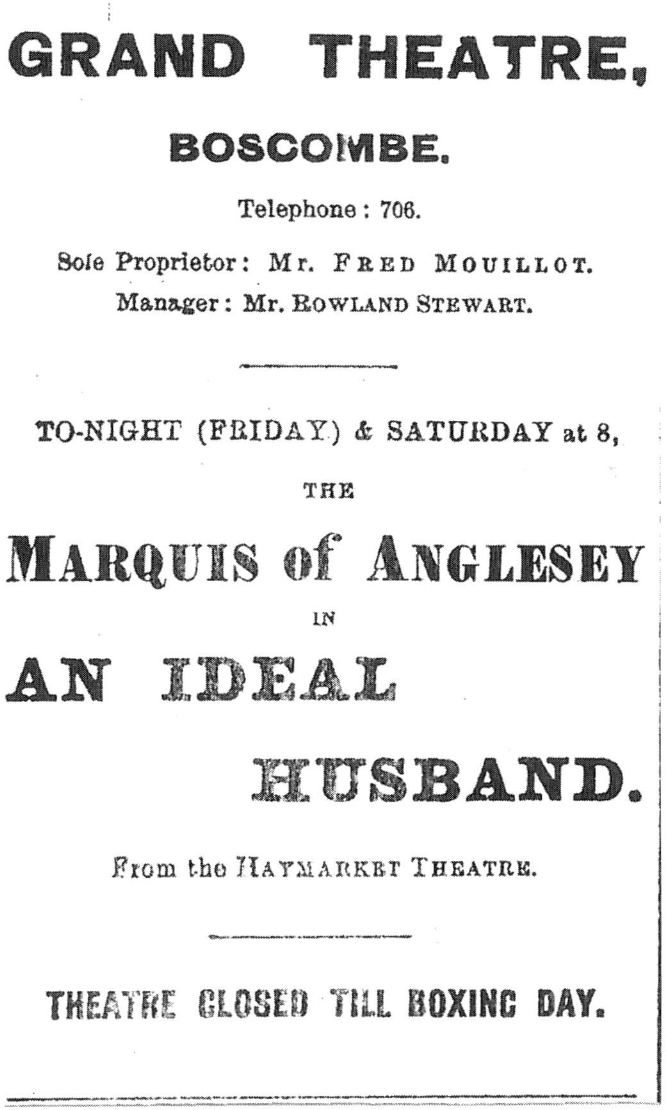

GRAND THEATRE,

BOSCOMBE.

Telephone : 706.

Sole Proprietor : Mr. FRED MOUILLOT.
Manager : Mr. ROWLAND STEWART.

TO-NIGHT (FRIDAY) & SATURDAY at 8,

THE

MARQUIS of ANGLESEY

IN

AN IDEAL

HUSBAND.

From the HAYMARKET THEATRE.

THEATRE CLOSED TILL BOXING DAY.

Fig. 15   Advert for the Marquis of Anglesey's *An Ideal Husband* (from the *Bournemouth Observer and Chronicle*, 27 November 1903).

Once again the staging and music earned the greatest praise:

> It is beautifully staged throughout, and it is some time since I
> have heard such exquisite music at a theatre. Mr Teague Crossley
> is to be highly complimented on his orchestra from Anglesey
> Castle, amalgamated with the theatre orchestra.

The following week, in Leamington Spa, where the Marquis as Lord
Goring, "portrayed the peculiar combination of foppish weakness and an
intimate knowledge of human nature with much skill." Indeed, there is
little criticism of the Marquis's acting throughout the tour, although the
Chicago Daily Tribune reported that he did "well on stage, save for difficulty
with his "r's," which usually take the sound of "w's."

The rest of the cast merited very little mention in most reviews: in
Bedford in the week leading to Christmas 1903 Gerald Alexander (Earl
of Caversham) "gives a clever character sketch," Miss Florence Tyrell (Lady
Chiltern) "presents a fine portrayal of an affectionate wife," Miss Florence
Hamer is "a most capable exponent," as Mrs Cheveley and Florence
Tempest's acting is "pretty". Minor parts were "well looked after".

After Christmas things began to go wrong for the tour. On 30 December
the *Manchester Courier* reported under the headline "Poor Bedridden Lord
Goring":

> For the New Year's festivities, Southport was looking forward
> to the visit at the Opera House for a week of the Marquis of
> Anglesey, who was to take the part of Lord Goring in "An Ideal
> Husband." But the Marquis is indisposed in Paris, and has
> telegraphed wishing the company "every luck and success from
> poor, bedridden Lord Goring."

The management of the Opera House were clearly not impressed and
the performance did not take place. At the sale of the Marquis's effects
(reported in local papers in July 1904) the sum of £400 was claimed by
the Opera House, Southport. In April 1905 some of the costumes that
would have been worn in the production were sold by auction along with a
portrait of the Marquis in "theatrical character".

The management at the Theatre and Opera House in Burton on Trent
were more forgiving in the first week of January and the "disappointed"
people of Burton saw Cecil Newton in the role of Lord Goring. The
Marquis sent a telegram to his manager, Alexander Keith, asking him to
"convey to the people of Burton my sincere regret" that he couldn't be there.
From the local paper's review we get a sense of the Marquis's extravagant
staging:

The play is superbly staged, the scenery and dresses never having been equalled in the matter of richness of quality on the Burton stage. In the first act ... a genuine Louis XV suite is used, while the electrically lit chandelier is re-modelled from the one in the yellow drawing-room at Beaudesert, the Marquis's seat situated between Lichfield and Rugeley. Lord Goring's rooms... are furnished with a remarkably fine suite of Chippendale furniture. In Act 2 a solid silver tea service, with costly china, is used at the afternoon tea, and the ornaments – which include some real Benares vases – are of a most valuable nature. The scenery is specially built, the pictures being real paintings executed in oils.

The Anglesey Castle orchestra provided a "musical treat", not only in the intervals, "but also during the performance in the "Music Room" at Sir Robert Chiltern's house."

Performances in Harrogate, York and Norwich, still without the Marquis, appear to have gone smoothly with a full house reported in Norwich for the first night of the week's run. Cecil Newton was thought to be an admirable replacement for the Marquis. In mid-February a visit to Huddersfield demonstrated the problems of modern technology.

A sudden failure of the public electric light service at Huddersfield about 7.45 last evening caused some inconvenience, besides being rather startling in places of public resort. At the Theatre Royal, the first act of "An Ideal Husband," being performed by the Marquis of Anglesey's Company, was got through by the aid of candles on the stage, and then the people had to be dismissed, and tickets for admission on another night were given to them. At the Empire Theatre the second turns had to be abandoned.

On 17 February 1904 *The Stage* announced

The Marquess [sic] of Anglesey has finished his provincial tour and performances were resumed at Anglesey Castle last night (Wednesday) with a representation of An Ideal Husband.

By now the estate was bankrupt and the *Sunderland Daily Echo* reported in July:

Referring to the denial of the statement that a huge discovery of jewellery has been made at Anglesey Castle, the Bangor correspondent of the Liverpool "Daily Post" maintains that a valuable "find" is in existence, and avers that one of the principal creditors of the Marquis of Anglesey confirms this. The creditor added that the recent discoveries mean the payment to all creditors of at least 10s in the £ within a couple of months. Over 300 fancy waistcoats belonging to the Marquis of Anglesey have been found at the Castle.

Amongst the Bangor creditors are three jewellers to whom he owes £26,651, £8,500, and £4,917; a stationer and printer, £2,000; and a "hairdresser, tobacconist, and dealer in gramophones," £285. The sum of £200 is due to the Queen's Theatre, Manchester, probably for failing to appear with "The Ideal Husband" Company, and £400 is claimed by the Opera House, Southport. One significant item is "Gampers, Monte Carlo", £1000." To Mr Alex. Keith, "theatrical manager to the Marquis of Anglesey," £4,786 is due.

By this time the Marquis was living in Monte Carlo on an income of £3,000 a year. He died the following year. Some stage properties intended for the performance that never was at Southport had been sent to the theatre in advance and were auctioned after his death. His theatrical manager, Alex Keith, who had been owed so much money by the Marquis, told the *North Wales Chronicle*, shortly after his death

Oh yes. In "The Marriage of Kitty" he was admitted by some capital critics to be distinctly good. But the best thing he did was "An Ideal Husband." The part might have been written for him; he went through it so naturally.

The Hartley tour of *Lady Windermere's Fan* continued beyond the end of the Marquis's tour, finishing in August 1904. In November George Alexander was at last confident enough to put Wilde's name on the adverts for the return of *Lady Windermere's Fan* to the St James's. However, he may not still have had complete confidence; the *Western Daily Press*, a week before the first night, said:

To-morrow week Mr Alexander revives Oscar Wilde's wonderful play, "Lady Windermere's Fan." It is understood that the author's name will not be on the play-bills and programmes. It seems somewhat hypocritical, especially when "The Woman without a Smile" is drawing big houses. It has been suggested that there be a season of Wilde revivals; it would undoubtedly show some of our essentially modern playwrights in a very bad light. The remarkable thing about Wilde's wit was that the superficial ring of it hid from the thoughtless a depth of philosophy. A complete edition of Wilde's works would be even more welcome than a series of revivals.

In the event, Wilde's name did appear on the programme. Three of the original cast played the roles they had played in 1892: Mr A Vane-

Tempest (always known by the single initial – his first names were Francis Adolphus) as Charles Dumby; Miss Fanny Coleman as the Duchess of Berwick; and Marion Terry as Mrs Erlynne. George Alexander did not appear. The curtain raiser was *The Decree Nisi* by Joshua Bates. There was a ten minute interval between each of the four acts. Patrons will have been reassured by the line in the programme which told them

The Scenery in this Theatre has been rendered fireproof by
the NON-FLAMMABLE WOOD FABRICS Co., Ltd

The audience for the first night included the Duchess of Marlborough and it was in aid of the West Ham Hospital Extension Fund. *The Manchester Courier* recorded that the "reception of the piece last night was flattering in its extreme cordiality". The play lasted until February the following year, with ninety five performances in all.

The week after the opening, the *Western Daily Press* demonstrated how comfortable they felt with Wilde's works by headlining a letter from the Archbishop of Canterbury "Church Defence; Letter from the Primate; The Importance of Being Earnest".

There was little activity in the early part of 1905, although two amateur performances of *The Importance of Being Earnest* at St Chad's Home, Far Headingley, Leeds were notable for including a Miss Fairfax among the cast. Interest in Wilde at this time, however, was focused on the publication of *De Profundis* and the *Western Daily Press* noted the law of (possibly) unintended consequences

It is a curious fact that upon the publication of a posthumous work the prices of the author's previous books go up. An inevitable result of the publication of "De Profundis" and the consequent re-awakening of interest in the author's personality, is the great demand for complete copies of Oscar Wilde's works. Second-hand booksellers have the field to themselves, as, for various reasons, it appears that no publisher is likely to issue a reasonably-priced edition of Wilde's novels, poems, essays, and plays.

There follows some detailed information about prices, and a rare mention of another of Wilde's plays

In France and Germany Oscar Wilde is looked upon as one of the masters of literature, and his works have a great sale, notably "Salome." So far this religious drama has not been seen in London, but next month the New Stage Club give a private performance of it, since the Censor has not passed it.

It was not just second-hand booksellers who took advantage; on 14 July 1905 it was reported that

> In the Chancery Division, to-day, before Mr Justice Swinfen Eady, Mr Frank Russell stated that he had a motion by Mr George Alexander, the well-known actor and manager, to restrain Wright and Jones, booksellers, Fulham, from infringing the copyright of the plaintiff in the book or play, called "Lady Windermere's Fan," written by the late Mr Oscar Wilde. What the defendant had done was to import into England a pirated edition of "Lady Windermere's Fan" printed in Paris. Mr Tomlin appeared for the defendant, and said he was willing to submit to the injunction. Negotiations were now proceeding for the settlement of this matter finally, and claims in respect of the other books. His Lordship made the order asked.

Despite this interest and openness about Wilde, some still hedged their bets. In March the Percy Standing company had put on *An Ideal Husband* at the Pier Pavilion in Hastings. A local paper, in the course of sixteen lines, described this both as "by the author of 'Lady Windermere's Fan'" and as "by the late Oscar Wilde".

The major tour of 1905 was of *An Ideal Husband*; it started at the Coronet Theatre in Notting Hill and Charles Ricketts's description began this chapter. What Ricketts calls, dismissively, a "provincial company" was the Herbert Dansey company and on that first night a "crowded audience" which included Sir Charles Wyndham, "demonstrated in no half-hearted manner its marked appreciation of the witty, sparkling dialogue and distinction of style which the able efforts of the excellent company brought out so admirably. Dansey gave "an unconventional and telling study of Viscount Goring, and is to be congratulated on his natural and unforced methods". George Bealby, an old Etonian married to Mabel Beardsley, "does well as the old Earl of Caversham, with the exception that his movements are a little juvenile as compared with those one would expect to be in keeping with his make-up"; Bealby was thirty at the time. Lionel Glenister, who played Phipps, was singled out for praise "for the manner in which he has rehearsed the company and performed the arduous duties of stage manager."

Charlotte Granville, who played Lady Chiltern in this production was at one time married to Major Robert Millington Synge, uncle of the playwright, J M Synge. She made a number of films in the 1930s, including *Werewolf of London*, in which she played Lady Forsythe.

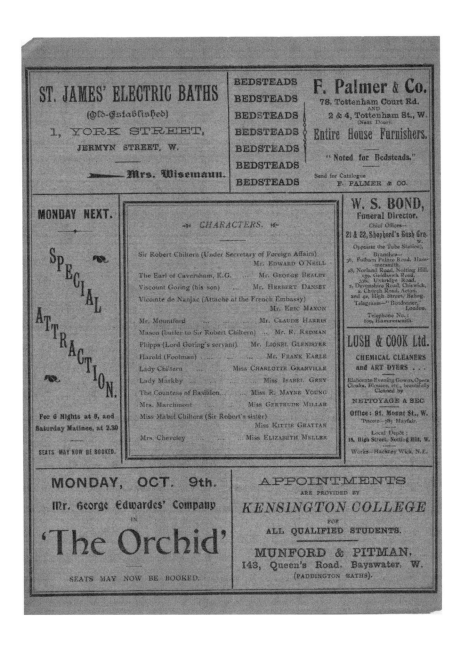

Fig. 16. *An Ideal Husband*, Coronet Theatre, Notting Hill, 1905. RHC RW/11/1/4/1 RHUL Archives.

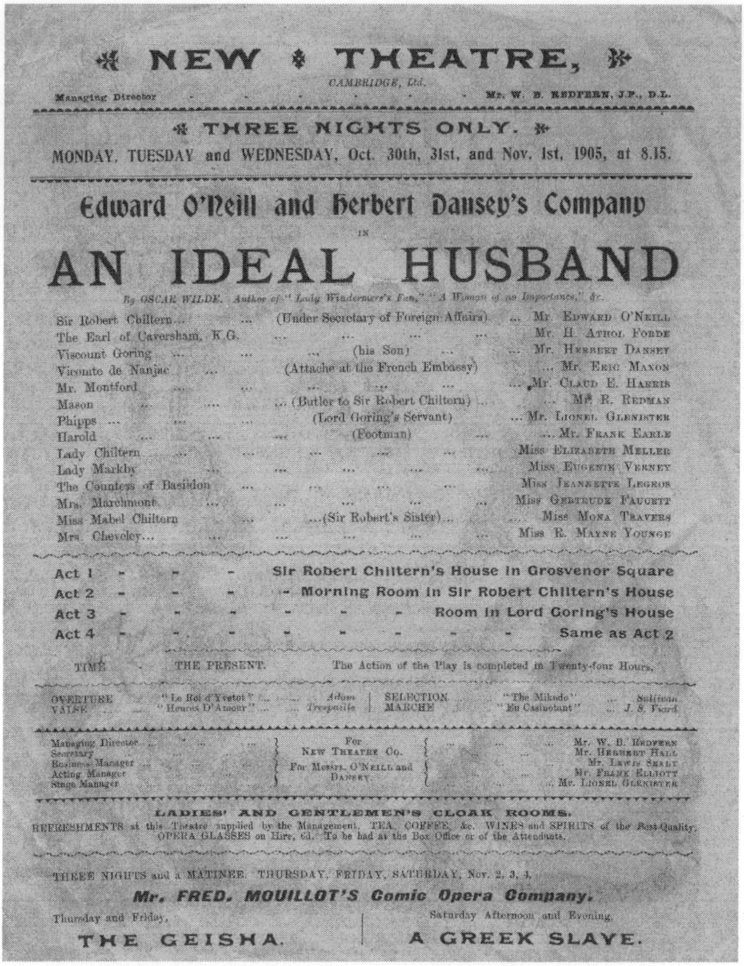

NEW THEATRE,

CAMBRIDGE, Ltd.

Managing Director . . . . Mr. W. B. Redfern, J.P., D.L.

THREE NIGHTS ONLY.

MONDAY, TUESDAY and WEDNESDAY, Oct. 30th, 31st, and Nov. 1st, 1905, at 8.15.

Edward O'Neill and Herbert Dansey's Company

IN

AN IDEAL HUSBAND

By OSCAR WILDE. Author of "Lady Windermere's Fan," "A Woman of no Importance," &c.

Sir Robert Chiltern	(Under Secretary of Foreign Affairs) ...	Mr. Edward O'Neill
The Earl of Caversham, K.G.	... ...	Mr. H. Athol Forde
Viscount Goring	... (his Son) ...	... Mr. Herbert Dansey
Vicomte de Nanjac ...	(Attache at the French Embassy)	... Mr. Eric Maxon
Mr. Montford	... ...	... Mr. Claud E. Harris
Mason	... (Butler to Sir Robert Chiltern) ...	... Mr. R. Redman
Phipps	(Lord Goring's Servant)	... Mr. Lionel Glenister
Harold	... (Footman) ...	... Mr. Frank Earle
Lady Chiltern	... ...	Miss Elizabeth Meller
Lady Markby ...	... ...	Miss Eugenie Verney
The Countess of Basildon ...	... ...	Miss Jeannette Legros
Mrs. Marchmont ...	... ...	Miss Gertrude Faucett
Miss Mabel Chiltern ...	...(Sir Robert's Sister)...	... Miss Mona Travers
Mrs. Cheveley... ...	... ...	Miss R. Mayne Younge

Act 1 - - - Sir Robert Chiltern's House in Grosvenor Square
Act 2 - - - - Morning Room in Sir Robert Chiltern's House
Act 3 - - - - - - Room in Lord Goring's House
Act 4 - - - - - - - - Same as Act 2

TIME - THE PRESENT. The Action of the Play is completed in Twenty-four Hours.

OVERTURE ... "Le Roi d'Yvetot" ... ... Adam | SELECTION ... "The Mikado" ... Sullivan
VALSE ... ... "Heures D'Amour" ... ... Trepsaile | MARCHE ... "En Casinotant" ... J. S. Vard

Managing Director ... Secretary ... } For New Theatre Co. { ... Mr. W. B. Redfern, Mr. Herbert Hall
Business Manager ... Acting Manager ... Stage Manager ... } For Messrs. O'Neill and Dansey. { ... Mr. Lewis Shalt, Mr. Frank Elliott, Mr. Lionel Glenister

LADIES' AND GENTLEMEN'S CLOAK ROOMS.

REFRESHMENTS at this Theatre supplied by the Management. TEA, COFFEE, &c. WINES and SPIRITS of the Best Quality.
OPERA GLASSES on Hire, 6d. To be had at the Box Office or of the Attendants.

THREE NIGHTS and a MATINEE. THURSDAY, FRIDAY, SATURDAY, Nov. 2, 3, 4,

Mr. FRED. MOUILLOT'S Comic Opera Company.

Thursday and Friday, THE GEISHA. | Saturday Afternoon and Evening, A GREEK SLAVE.

Fig. 17 *An Ideal Husband*, New Theatre, Cambridge, 1905. Private Collection.

Herbert Dansey's first appearance on stage had been as Lane in Alexander's touring production of *The Importance of Being Earnest* in 1901 and then at the St James's theatre. Dansey was his stage name; his given name was Count Berto Danyell Tassinari and he had been born in Florence. He was a writer and painter as well, and in 1902 had held a joint exhibition with Alessandro Guaccimanni of "pictures of sunny Italy" at the Continental Gallery in London. This tour appears to have been his first with his own company and although he played in a number of West-End productions he went to America where he toured in a production of Shaw's

Fanny's First Play and made a number of films. He died in New York in 1917.

There is no record of any professional productions during 1906 but amateur productions were staged in London and Birmingham. The last major tour of this period began in May 1907; the Monckton Hoffe (or Hoffe and Campbell) company took *The Importance of Being Earnest* around the country for the rest of 1907 and into the following year. Hoffe had been born in Ireland and at this time was only twenty seven. He later became much better known as a playwright and screenwriter, collaborating in Hollywood with, among others, Preston Sturges. During World War II he wrote propaganda films. At the beginning of July 1907 the Yorkshire Post reported:

> So well has the revival of "The Importance of Being Earnest" been received in the provinces that Mr Monckton Hoffe, who, when he was in Leeds a few weeks ago, told me he was considering a revival of "Lady Windermere's Fan," has now decided to add this brilliant comedy to his repertoire.

Wilde's name was on the adverts for this tour, and the reviewers seem to have had no difficulty mentioning him. However, opinions were divided about the production. In Southport the cast were uniformly praised but in Hull there was a more measured approach

> It must be more than ten years since Hull playgoers had the opportunity of seeing Oscar Wilde's play, *The Importance of Being Earnest*, and on this account alone the chance of renewing acquaintance with this cleverly written comedy should prove of interest. Mr Moncton Hoffe is seen in the part of Algernon Moncrieff, a character in which he appears quite at home. Mr C Nicholson is not altogether happy as John Worthing J P. Mr Ralph Hutton is suitably placed as the Rev Canon Chasuble. Miss Winnie Grey as the Hon Gwendoline Fairfax is too stilted in her manner. Miss Heston Newton makes an acceptable Cecily Cardew. Miss Amy Lloyd-Desmond is sufficiently firm as Miss Prism.

Not a word about Lady Bracknell (in Southport the actress playing her was summed up as "austere"). In York "The opportunity of relief from the succession of musical comedies was welcomed by a large audience," and in Tunbridge Wells they had to put on an extra matinee of *Lady Windermere's Fan* by popular request. The curtain raiser was *A Queen's Messenger*. The next town on the tour was Sheffield, however, where, in an otherwise good review of the play, the *Sheffield Independent* said:

The revival of Oscar Wilde's "Lady Windermere's Fan" has evidently not impressed playgoers in Sheffield so favourably as in some other places, and the consequence was that last night the Lyceum Theatre was sparsely filled when the Monckton Hoffe Comedy Company presented the piece.

In December the Monckton Hoffe Comedy Company was performing *His Excellency the Governor* (which they had been touring with *Lady Windermere*) in Manchester, but they returned to *Earnest* in February 1908 at the Scala Theatre in London and the tour appears to have continued well into the year with dates in Belfast and Harrogate.

Part way through the Monckton tour, the Ernest E Norris company started to tour *An Ideal Husband*. This appears to have been less a tour and more a few separate dates from May to November.

By the time the Monckton Hoffe tour ended in March 1908, Robert Ross had reunited Wilde's copyrights and, in February 1908, had published the first six volumes of the first collected edition of the works of Oscar Wilde. In mid-October the last two volumes of the fourteen volume set were published and, on 1 December a "Complimentary Dinner to Mr Robert Ross" was held at the Ritz Hotel in London to celebrate their publication.[7]

According to the *Times* the next day

> The Chairman [Sir Martin Conway], after submitting the loyal toasts, announced that the gathering was composed of 36 journalists and critics, five actors, 11 art connoisseurs, five Government officials, 20 authors, four editors, 12 poets, four dramatists, seven artists, four publishers, four men of science and medicine, two clergy, four lawyers, and many other people whom he could "not put into a definite category." (Laughter)

Actors were not mentioned, although Mabel Beardsley was there and George Alexander arrived late (Beerbohm Tree sent his regrets), but that list would seem to indicate that Wilde's rehabilitation – at least at a certain level of society – was complete.

Ross gave a speech at that dinner in the opening lines of which he acknowledged that Wilde's plays had continued to be performed

> I once attended a provincial performance of Wilde's play "A Woman of No Importance". You may possibly remember from

---

7 *Bibliography of Oscar Wilde*, by Stuart Mason. T Werner Laurie 1914, p. 459.

Mr Tree's brilliant revival the curtain in Act III which falls on the exclamation of Mrs Arbuthnot "Don't strike him Gerald he is your father." At this performance the manager, he was an actor-manager, fearing that the text was inadequate, fearing that the curtain would not sufficiently impress the house, had instructed the leading artist to turn to the audience with her outstretched arms and this gagged aside "What a situation".

APPENDIX I

DATES AND PLAYS

Dates given here are, where possible, for the first performance of a play during a company's visit to the theatre. In many cases it has not been possible to establish the order of performance from a repertory of plays, in which case the date given is for the first day of the engagement.

It has not been possible to positively identify theatres in all cases; where an informed guess can be made it appears in square brackets. Where appropriate the touring classification is given beside the name of the theatre. These are taken from *The Green Room Book for 1907* and indicate first, second or third class, or "fit-up" theatres. As they apply to touring theatres, none of those within the Greater London area have classifications.

1895

JANUARY

3	AIH	Waller & M	London (Haymarket Theatre)
3	WoNI	Morell & M	Shrewsbury (Theatre Royal)
7	WoNI	Morell & M	York (Theatre Royal)
10	WoNI	Morell & M	Tunbridge Wells [Opera House] 3
17	WoNI	Morell & M	Durham (Assembly Rooms) fit-up
24	WoNI	Morell & M	Lancaster (Athenaeum Theatre)
28	WoNI	Morell & M	Stockton (Theatre Royal) 3

FEBRUARY

4	WoNI	Morell & M	Workington (Queen's Opera House)
11	WoNI	Morell & M	South Shields (Theatre Royal) 3
11	LWF	Olga Brandon	Camberwell (Metropole Theatre)
14	IoBE	Alexander	London (St James's Theatre)
18	WoNI	Morell & M	Hartlepool (Theatre Royal)
25	WoNI	Morell & M	Barrow in Furness (Royalty Theatre)

MARCH

4	WoNI	Morell & M	London (Bishopsgate Institute Theatre)
11	WoNI	Morell & M	London (Parkhurst Theatre)
18	WoNI	Morell & M	Cardiff (Theatre Royal) 1
25	WoNI	Morell & M	Swansea (New Theatre)
28	AIH	Waller & M	London (Crystal Palace)

APRIL

4	IoBE	Alexander	Brighton (Theatre Royal) 1
13	AIH	Waller & M	London (Criterion Theatre)
15	WoNI	Morell & M	Merthyr Tydfil (Royal and Opera House)
22	WoNI	Morell & M	Newport (Victoria Theatre)

MAY

2	WoNI	Morell & M	Bath (Theatre Royal) 2
6	WoNI	Morell & M	Birkenhead (Metropole Theatre)
13	WoNI	Morell & M	Halifax (Grand Theatre) 3
27	WoNI	Morell & M	Doncaster [New Grand] 3
30	WoNI	Morell & M	Gloucester (Theatre Royal) 3

JUNE

3	WoNI	Morell & M	Exeter (Theatre Royal) 2
10	WoNI	Morell & M	Worcester (Theatre Royal) 3
10	AIH	Sarah Thorne	Margate (Theatre Royal) 3

JULY

1	AIH	Waller & M	London (Grand Theatre)

SEPTEMBER

23	AIH	Waller & M	London (Morton's Model Theatre)

2	IoBE	Tapping	Kidderminster (Theatre Royal)
7	AIH	Waller & M	Ryde (Theatre Royal) 3
8	IoBE	Tapping	Stourbridge (New Alhambra Theatre)
Nd	IoBE	Tapping	Stafford (Lyceum Theatre)
18	IoBE	Tapping	Walsall (Grand Theatre)
21	IoBE	Tapping	Cork (Opera House) 2
28	IoBE	Tapping	Limerick (Theatre Royal)
Nd	IoBE	Tapping	Waterford (Theatre Royal)

NOVEMBER

4	IoBE	Tapping	Blackpool (New Grand Theatre) 2
Nd	IoBE	Tapping	Folkestone (Pleasure Gardens) 2
27	IoBE	Tapping	Grimsby (Prince of Wales Theatre) 2

DECEMBER

16	AIH	Hawtrey	London (Lyric Theatre)
16	IoBE	Tapping	London (Metropole Theatre)

1896

JANUARY

27	IoBE	Tapping	Limerick (Theatre Royal)

FEBRUARY

3	IoBE	Tapping	Waterford (Theatre Royal)
17	IoBE	Tapping	Ipswich (Lyceum Theatre) 3
27	WoNI	Varna	Bath (Theatre Royal) 2

MARCH

2	WoNI	Varna	Wells (Town Hall) fit-up
23	WoNI	Varna	Nuneaton (Theatre Royal) 3
30	WoNI	Varna	Market Harborough (New Hall) fit-up

APRIL

| 1 | WoNI | Varna | Grantham (Theatre Royal) |

MAY

| 18 | WoNI | Varna | Grimsby (Prince of Wales Theatre) 2 |
| 25 | WoNI | Varna | Macclesfield (Theatre Royal) |

JULY

13	AIH	Hawtrey	Newcastle upon Tyne (Theatre Royal) 1
20	AIH	Hawtrey	Brighton(Theatre Royal) 1
27	AIH	Hawtrey	London (Parkhurst Theatre)

AUGUST

3	AIH	Hawtrey	Leamington (New Theatre Royal)
10	AIH	Hawtrey	Liverpool (Court Theatre) 1
13	WoNI	Varna	Matlock Bank (Theatre Hall)
17	AIH	Hawtrey	Manchester (Prince's Theatre) 1
31	WoNI	Varna	Lytham (Pier Pavilion) fit-up

SEPTEMBER

7	AIH	Hawtrey	Middlesborough (Theatre Royal) 2
10	WoNI	Varna	Wrexham (St James's Theatre) fit-up
14	AIH	Hawtrey	Harrogate [Opera House] 2
17	AIH	Hawtrey	Matlock (Pavilion Theatre)
21	WoNI	Varna	Devonport (Metropole Theatre) 2
21	AIH	Hawtrey	Great Yarmouth (Theatre Royal)
28	AIH	Hawtrey	Northampton (Opera House) 2

OCTOBER

1	AIH	Hawtrey	Blackburn(Theatre Royal) 3
5	AIH	Hawtrey	Glasgow (Royalty Theatre) 1
12	WoNI	Varna	Merthyr Tydfil (New Theatre)
12	AIH	Hawtrey	Inverness [Theatre Royal]

15	AIH	Hawtrey	Dumfries [Theatre Royal]
19	AIH	Hawtrey	Edinburgh (Theatre Royal) 1
26	AIH	Hawtrey	Scarborough (Londesborough Theatre) 2
29	LWF	Myrlyn	Colchester (Theatre Royal) 3

NOVEMBER

2	AIH	Hawtrey	Dublin (Gaiety Theatre) 1
7	LWF	Myrlyn	Bournemouth (Theatre Royal) 2
9	AIH	Hawtrey	Cork (Opera House) 2
9	LWF	Myrlyn	Maidenhead (Grand Hall) fit-up
16	AIH	Hawtrey	Manchester (Prince's Theatre) 1
16	LWF	Myrlyn	Bury (Theatre Royal)
23	LWF	Myrlyn	Ipswich (Lyceum Theatre) 3
23	AIH	Hawtrey	Newcastle upon Tyne (Theatre Royal) 1
30	LWF	Myrlyn	Norwich (Theatre Royal) 3
30	AIH	Hawtrey	Preston (Theatre Royal) 3

DECEMBER

7	LWF	Myrlyn	Great Yarmouth (Theatre Royal)
7	AIH	Hawtrey	Blackburn (Theatre Royal) 3
14	AIH	Hawtrey	Hammersmith (Lyric Opera House)
17	AIH	Hawtrey	London (New Ealing Theatre)

1897

FEBRUARY

12	WoNI	Morell & M	London (Theatre Royal, Kilburn)
16	IoBE	Tapping	Grimsby (Prince of Wales Theatre) 2
21	IoBE	Tapping	Belfast (Theatre Royal) 1
25	WoNI	Morell & M	Bournemouth (Theatre Royal) 2

MARCH

| 1 | IoBE | Tapping | Hastings (Pier Pavilion) |

APRIL

12   LWF   Bandman   Hastings (Pier Pavilion)

AUGUST

5   IoBE   Tapping   Clacton (Operetta House)

1898

MAY

15   LWF   Cressy   Brighton (West Pier)

JUNE

3   WoNI   Homer   Halifax (Theatre Royal) 3

JULY

25   WoNI   Homer   Bradford (Prince's Theatre) 1

AUGUST

1   WoNI   Homer   Dewsbury (Theatre Royal)
8   WoNI   Homer   Smethwick [Theatre Royal]
29   WoNI   Homer   Derby (Grand Theatre) 2

SEPTEMBER

12   WoNI   Homer   Sheffield (Alexandra Theatre) 2
26   WoNI   Homer   Leeds (Theatre Royal) 2

OCTOBER

3   WoNI   Homer   Oldham (Empire Theatre)
17   WoNI   Homer   Consett (Theatre Royal)
24   WoNI   Homer   Rochdale (Theatre Royal) 3
31   WoNI   Homer   Wigan(Court Theatre) 2

3	WoNI	Homer	Keighley (Queen's Theatre)
7	WoNI	Homer	Bilston (Theatre Royal) 3
10	WoNI	Homer	Preston (Theatre Royal) 3
28	WoNI	Homer	Manchester (Queen's Theatre) 2

DECEMBER

5	WoNI	Homer	Doncaster (Opera House)
26	WoNI	Homer	Gravesend (Public Hall) fit-up

1899

JANUARY

2	WoNI	Homer	Margate (Grand Theatre) 2
9	WoNI	Homer	Eastbourne (Theatre Royal)
16	WoNI	Homer	Swansea (Grand Theatre)
23	WoNI	Homer	Llanelli (Royalty Theatre)
30	WoNI	Homer	Dudley (Colosseum Theatre

FEBRUARY

13	WoNI	Homer	Accrington (Prince's Theatre) 3
20	WoNI	Homer	Lancaster (Theatre Royal)

MARCH

6	WoNI	Homer	Blackpool (Her Majesty's Theatre) 2
13	WoNI	Homer	Bedford Leigh (Theatre Royal)
23	WoNI	Homer	Great Yarmouth (Aquarium Theatre) 2
23	IoBE	Tapping	Hastings (Pier Pavilion)
27	WoNI	Homer	London (Queen's Theatre, Crouch End)

APRIL

3	WoNI	Homer	Boscombe (Grand Theatre)
10	WoNI	Homer	Cambridge (New Theatre) 2
13	WoNI	Homer	Oxford (New Theatre) 2

| 17 | WoNI | Homer | Luton (Grand Theatre) |
| 24 | WoNI | Homer | Barrow in Furness (Royalty Theatre) |

MAY

1	WoNI	Homer	South Shields (Theatre Royal) 3
5	WoNI	Homer	Hastings (Gaiety Theatre) 2
8	WoNI	Homer	Jarrow (Theatre Royal) 3
12	WoNI	Homer	Birmingham (Grand Theatre) 1
15	WoNI	Homer	Darlington (Theatre Royal) 3
19	WoNI	Homer	Douglas (Grand Theatre) 2
22	WoNI	Homer	Grimsby (Prince of Wales Theatre) 2
26	WoNI	Homer	Southport (Opera House) 2

SEPTEMBER

| 18 | LWF | Lanham | Llanelli (Royalty Theatre) |

OCTOBER

9	LWF	Lanham	Stafford (Lyceum Theatre)
16	LWF	Lanham	Llandudno (New Prince's Theatre)
23	LWF	Lanham	Bootle (Royal Muncaster Theatre)
30	LWF	Lanham	Castleford (New Queen's Theatre)

NOVEMBER

16	LWF	Lanham	Crewe (Lyceum Theatre)
20	IoBE	Lanham	Scarborough (People's Palace)
27	IoBE	Lanham	Coventry (Royal Opera House) 2
30	WoNI	Waller	London (Coronet Theatre)
30	LWF	Lanham	Gloucester (Theatre Royal) 3

DECEMBER

4	LWF	Amateur	Glasgow (Athenaeum Theatre) fit-up
4	IoBE	Lanham	Southport (Opera House) 2
7	LWF	Lanham	Southport (Opera House) 2

11	IoBE	Lanham	Leamington (Theatre Royal)
14	LWF	Lanham	Glasgow (Athenaeum Theatre) fit-up
18	LWF	Lanham	Hastings (Gaiety Theatre) 2
21	IoBE	Lanham	Hastings (Gaiety Theatre) 2

1900

JANUARY

1	LWF	Lanham	Burton on Trent (St George's Theatre)
4	IoBE	Lanham	Burton on Trent (St George's Theatre)
6	IoBE	Lanham	Londonderry (Opera House)
22	IoBE	Lanham	Blackpool (Opera House) 2
29	LWF	Lanham	Belfast (Grand Opera House)

FEBRUARY

12	LWF	Amateur	London (St George's Hall)
19	LWF	Cressy	Margate (New Grand Theatre) 2
19	LWF	Lanham	Harrogate (Grand Opera House) 2
20	IoBE	Lanham	Harrogate (Grand Opera House) 2
23	LWF	Lanham	Grantham (Theatre Royal)
26	LWF	Cressy	Hastings (Pier Pavilion)
26	LWF	Lanham	London (Royal Artillery Theatre)

MARCH

5	LWF	Lanham	Blackburn (Theatre Royal) 3
6	IoBE	Lanham	Blackburn (Theatre Royal) 3
12	LWF	Lanham	Oxford (New Theatre) 2
19	WoNI	Waller	Manchester (Theatre Royal) 1
22	IoBE	Lanham	Eastbourne (Theatre Royal)
26	AIH	Cressy	Brighton (West Pier)
26	LWF	Lanham	Boscombe (Grand Theatre)
28	IoBE	Lanham	Boscombe (Grand Theatre)

APRIL

2	LWF	Cressy	Eastbourne (Theatre Royal)
2	LWF	Lanham	Shrewsbury (Theatre Royal)
3	IoBE	Lanham	Shrewsbury (Theatre Royal)
9	LWF	Lanham	Keighley (New Queen's Theatre)
16	AIH	Cressy	Kings Lynn (Theatre Royal) 2
16	LWF	Lanham	Hartlepool (Theatre Royal)
17	IoBE	Lanham	Hartlepool (Theatre Royal)
23	AIH	Cressy	Ipswich (Lyceum Theatre) 3
23	LWF	Lanham	South Shields [Theatre Royal] 3
28	LWF	Lanham	Scarborough (People's Palace)

MAY

7	AIH	Cressy	Margate (Grand Theatre) 3
18	AIH	Cressy	Dover (Theatre Royal)
19	WoNI	Homer	Southampton (New Grand Theatre) 2
24	AIH	Cressy	Brighton (West Pier)
28	LWF	Cressy	Brighton (West Pier)

JUNE

4	LWF	Lanham	Leigh (Theatre Royal)
28	LWF	Lanham	Preston (New Theatre Royal) 3

JULY

14	LWF	Lanham	Barrow in Furness (Royalty Theatre)
16	WoNI	Homer	Southend (Empire Theatre) 3
26	WoNI	Homer	Liverpool (Lyric Theatre) 2
30	WoNI	Homer	Halifax (Theatre Royal) 3

AUGUST

7	LWF	Lanham	Bridlington (Royal Victoria Theatre) fit up
10	LWF	Lanham	Whitby (West Cliff Saloon Theatre) fit up
13	WoNI	Homer	Keighley (Queen's Theatre)

13	IoBE	Tapping	Brighton (West Pier)
16	AIH	Cressy	Great Malvern (Assembly Rooms)
20	AIH	Cressy	Birmingham (Grand Theatre) 1
23	LWF	(unknown)	Ilkley (Victoria Theatre)
23	WoNI	Homer	Birkenhead (Metropole Theatre)
27	AIH	Cressy	Aberystwyth (Pier Theatre)
30	WoNI	Homer	Widnes (Alexandra Theatre)

SEPTEMBER

3	WoNI	Homer	Swansea (Grand Theatre)
6	AIH	Cressy	Shrewsbury (New Royal Theatre)
10	AIH	Cressy	Bridlington (Royal Victoria Theatre)
10	WoNI	Homer	Windsor [Theatre Royal]
10	LWF	Lanham	Peterborough (Theatre Royal)
13	AIH	Cressy	Lowestoft (Marina Theatre)
13	WoNI	Homer	Grantham (Theatre Royal)
18	WoNI	Homer	Seacombe (Irving Theatre)
20	AIH	Cressy	Clacton (Operetta House)
24	WoNI	Homer	Barrow in Furness (Royalty Theatre)
24	LWF	Lanham	Limerick (Theatre Royal)
27	AIH	Cressy	Lowestoft (Marina Theatre)

OCTOBER

1	WoNI	Homer	Morecambe (Royalty Theatre)
1	LWF	Lanham	Cork (Opera House) 2
1	LWF	Thalberg	Kennington (Prince of Wales Theatre)
4	AIH	Cressy	Scarborough (People's Palace)
8	LWF	Lanham	Torquay (Theatre Royal)
8	WoNI	Homer	Jersey (New Royal Theatre)
8	LWF	Thalberg	London (New Ealing Theatre)
12	WoNI	Homer	Guernsey (St Julian's Hall) fit-up
15	LWF	Thalberg	Bournemouth (Theatre Royal) 2
22	LWF	Thalberg	Nottingham (Theatre Royal) 1

| 25 | WoNI | Homer | Kingston (County Theatre) 2 |

1	WoNI	Homer	Hereford (Theatre Royal)
5	WoNI	Homer	Hanley (Theatre Royal) 2
5	LWF	Lanham	Bideford (Public Rooms) fit-up
5	LWF	Thalberg	London (Opera House, Crouch End)
12	LWF	Thalberg	Birmingham (Prince of Wales Theatre) 1
12	LWF	Lanham	Dover (Theatre Royal)
19	WoNI	Homer	Liverpool (Lyric Theatre) 2
19	LWF	Thalberg	Richmond [Prince of Wales]
26	WoNI	Homer	Blackpool (Opera House) 2
29	LWF	Amateur	Southport (Opera House and Winter Gardens) 2

DECEMBER

3	WoNI	Homer	Shrewsbury (Theatre Royal)
10	WoNI	Homer	St Albans (County Hall)
13	WoNI	Homer	Reading (Royal County Theatre) 2
26	LWF	Thalberg	Cork (Opera House) 2

1901

JANUARY

| 14 | LWF | Lanham | South Shields (Theatre Royal) 3 |

FEBRUARY

| 18 | LWF | Thalberg | London (Camden Theatre) |
| 28 | LWF | Thalberg | Bath (Theatre Royal) 2 |

MARCH

4	LWF	Thalberg	London (Coronet Theatre)
4	WoNI	Homer	Gloucester (Theatre Royal) 3
11	LWF	Thalberg	Northampton (Theatre Royal)

18	LWF	Thalberg	Belfast (Theatre Royal) 1
18	WoNI	Homer	Hastings (Pier Pavilion)
25	LWF	Thalberg	Hanley (Theatre Royal) 2

APRIL

1	LWF	Thalberg	Bristol (Prince's Theatre) 1
8	LWF	Thalberg	Cardiff (Theatre Royal) 1
8	WoNI	Homer	Kendal (St George's Hall)
15	LWF	Thalberg	London (Brixton Theatre)
22	WoNI	Homer	Glasgow (Metropole Theatre) 3
29	WoNI	Homer	Halifax (Theatre Royal) 3
29	LWF	Thalberg	London (Crown Theatre, Peckham)

MAY

6	LWF	Thalberg	Cambridge (New Theatre) 2
6	WoNI	Homer	Norwich (Theatre Royal) 3
13	WoNI	Homer	Dudley (Opera House)
13	LWF	Thalberg	Liverpool (Shakespeare Theatre) 1
20	WoNI	Homer	Eccles (Lyceum Theatre)
23	LWF	Klein	Bilston (Theatre Royal) 3
23	IoBE	Klein	Bilston (Theatre Royal) 3
27	WoNI	Homer	Darlington (Theatre Royal) 3
30	LWF	Klein	Wednesbury (Theatre Royal)
30	IoBE	Klein	Wednesbury (Theatre Royal)

JUNE

6	LWF	Klein	Chorley (Grand Theatre)
8	IoBE	Klein	Chorley (Grand Theatre)
10	WoNI	Homer	Bury (Theatre Royal) 3
13	LWF	Klein	Broughton (Victoria Theatre)
15	IoBE	Klein	Broughton (Victoria Theatre)
17	WoNI	Homer	Rochdale (Theatre Royal) 3
20	LWF	Klein	Greenwich (Morton's Model Theatre)

22	IoBE	Klein	London (Morton's Model Theatre)

JULY

29	LWF	Klein	Fleetwood (Queen's Theatre)

AUGUST

5	LWF	Klein	St Anne's (Public Hall Theatre) fit-up
8	IoBE	Klein	St Anne's (Public Hall Theatre) fit-up
15	LWF	Klein	Halifax (Theatre Royal) 3
18	IoBE	Klein	Halifax (Theatre Royal) 3
19	LWF	Klein	Accrington (Prince's Theatre) 3
22	IoBE	Klein	Accrington (Prince's Theatre) 3

SEPTEMBER

2	LWF	Klein	Wrexham (St James's Theatre) fit-up
5	IoBE	Klein	Wrexham (St James's Theatre) fit-up
9	LWF	Klein	Whitby (West Cliff Saloon) fit-up
10	IoBE	Klein	Whitby (West Cliff Saloon) fit-up
12	LWF	Klein	Goole (Theatre Royal)
16	LWF	Klein	Stafford (Lyceum Theatre)
19	IoBE	Klein	Stafford (Lyceum Theatre)
23	LWF	Klein	Aberystwyth (Pier Pavilion)
26	IoBE	Klein	Aberystwyth (Pier Pavilion)
30	LWF	Klein	Shrewsbury (Theatre Royal)

OCTOBER

3	IoBE	Klein	Shrewsbury (Theatre Royal)
7	IoBE	Klein	Doncaster (Grand Theatre) 3
9	LWF	Klein	Doncaster (Grand Theatre) 3
27	LWF	Klein	Bexhill (Kursaal)
28	IoBE	Alexander	Liverpool (Court Theatre) 1
29	IoBE	Klein	Bexhill (Kursaal)

NOVEMBER

4	IoBE	Alexander	Manchester (Theatre Royal) 1
4	LWF	Klein	Oxford (Empire Theatre)
6	IoBE	Klein	Oxford (Empire Theatre)
11	IoBE	Alexander	Belfast (Opera House)
18	IoBE	Alexander	Dublin (Theatre Royal) 1
28	IoBE	Alexander	Nottingham (Theatre Royal) 1

DECEMBER

2	IoBE	Alexander	London (Coronet Theatre)
9	IoBE	Alexander	Brighton (Theatre Royal) 1
16	IoBE	Alexander	London (Kennington Theatre)

1902

JANUARY

| 7 | IoBE | Alexander | London (St James's Theatre) |

FEBRUARY

| 21 | LWF | Amateur | Surbiton (Assembly Rooms) fit-up |

MARCH

| 1 | LWF | Amateur | Surbiton (Assembly Rooms) fit-up |
| 31 | IoBE | Weathersby | London (Crystal Palace Theatre) |

APRIL

| 2 | AIH | Cressy | Drogheda (Whitworth Hall) fit-up |

MAY

| 8 | AIH | Cressy | Brighton (West Pier) |
| 14 | AIH | Amateur | Reading (Royal County Theatre) 2 |

JULY

| 11 | IoBE | Hare | Great Yarmouth (Theatre Royal) |

24	IoBE	Hare	Scarborough (Londesborough Theatre) 2

AUGUST

4	IoBE	Hare	Gloucester (Theatre Royal) 3
25	WoNI	Cooke	Croydon (Grand Theatre)

SEPTEMBER

1	WoNI	Cooke	Great Yarmouth (Theatre Royal)
8	WoNI	Cooke	Norwich (Theatre Royal) 3
15	WoNI	Cooke	Lincoln (Theatre Royal) 3
22	WoNI	Cooke	Scarborough (Spa Theatre)

OCTOBER

2	WoNI	Cooke	Bridlington (Royal Victoria Theatre)
6	WoNI	Cooke	Limerick (Theatre Royal)
16	WoNI	Cooke	Cork (Opera House) 2
20	WoNI	Cooke	Brighton (West Pier)
27	WoNI	Cooke	Folkestone (Pleasure Gardens) 2

NOVEMBER

3	WoNI	Cooke	Eastbourne (Pier Theatre)
10	WoNI	Cooke	Walsall (Her Majesty's Theatre)
17	WoNI	Cooke	Liverpool (Prince of Wales Theatre)

DECEMBER

8	WoNI	Cooke	Dublin (Gaiety Theatre)
12	WoNI	Cooke	Brighton (West Pier)
15	WoNI	Cooke	Swansea (Grand Theatre)
15	LWF	Amateur	Camberwell (Surrey Masonic Hall)

1903

JANUARY

27	IoBE	Amateur	London (Imperial Theatre, Westminster)

MARCH

| 6 | IoBE | Amateur | Manchester (Athenaeum Theatre) |
| 7 | AIH | Amateur | London (Regent Street Polytechnic) |

MAY

| 9 | IoBE | Amateur | London (Regent Street Polytechnic |
| 18 | IoBE | Hare | Dublin (Gaiety Theatre) 1 |

JUNE

6	IoBE	Pardoe	Teddington (The Bijou Theatre) fit-up
8	IoBE	Hare	Cardiff (Theatre Royal) 1
19	IoBE	Hare	Bristol (Prince's Theatre) 1
20	IoBE	Pardoe	Folkestone (Pleasure Gardens)

JULY

| 27 | IoBE | Pardoe | Torquay (Theatre Royal) |

AUGUST

| 17 | WoNI | Hartley | London (Crystal Palace) |

SEPTEMBER

| 23 | WoNI | Hartley | London (Empire Theatre, Balham) |
| 28 | WoNI | Hartley | Bury St Edmunds (Theatre Royal) |

OCTOBER

5	WoNI	Hartley	Gainsborough (Theatre Royal)
12	WoNI	Hartley	Loughborough (Town Hall)
19	WoNI	Hartley	Windsor (Theatre Royal)
22	WoNI	Hartley	Newmarket (Victoria Theatre) fit-up
26	WoNI	Hartley	Oldham (Coliseum Theatre)

4	WoNI	Hartley	Boscombe (Grand Theatre)
6	LWF	Hartley	Boscombe (Grand Theatre)
9	WoNI	Hartley	Margate (Grand Theatre) 2
23	AIH	Anglesey	Lichfield (St James's Hall) fit-up
30	AIH	Anglesey	Boscombe (Grand Theatre)
30	LWF	Amateur	Manchester (Midland Hall)
30	LWF	Hartley	Blackpool (Opera House) 2

DECEMBER

2	WoNI	Hartley	Blackpool (Opera House) 2
7	LWF	Hartley	Brighton (Palace Pier Pavilion)
7	AIH	Anglesey	Folkestone (Pleasure Gardens) 2
9	WoNI	Hartley	Brighton (Palace Pier Pavilion)
14	AIH	Anglesey	Leamington (New Royal Theatre)
24	AIH	Anglesey	Bedford (Royal County Theatre)
26	WoNI	Hartley	Bexhill (Kursaal)
31	AIH	Anglesey	Southport (Opera House) 2

1904

JANUARY

11	AIH	Anglesey	Harrogate (Kursaal)
14	AIH	Anglesey	York (Theatre Royal) 2
19	LWF	Hartley	Folkestone (Pleasure Gardens)

FEBRUARY

1	LWF	Hartley	London (Crystal Palace)
4	AIH	Anglesey	Norwich (Grand Opera House) 3
11	AIH	Anglesey	Huddersfield (Theatre Royal) 3
17	AIH	Anglesey	Beaumaris (Anglesey Castle)
18	LWF	Hartley	Southend (Pier Pavilion)
22	AIH	not known	Hull (Theatre Royal) 1

APRIL

| 11 | LWF | Hartley | Jersey (Opera House) |
| 26 | LWF | Hartley | Dover (Theatre Royal) |

MAY

| 4 | IoBE | Hare | Cambridge (New Theatre) 2 |
| 9 | LWF | Hartley | Worthing (Theatre Royal) 3 |

JUNE

| 6 | IoBE | Hare | Cheltenham (Opera House) 2 |
| 9 | IoBE | Amateur | Cambridge (New Theatre) 2 |

JULY

| 7 | LWF | Hartley | Scarborough (The Spa) |

AUGUST

| 8 | AIH | not known | Hull (Grand Theatre) |
| 8 | LWF | not known | Hull (Grand Theatre) |

OCTOBER

| 10 | LWF | not known | Hastings (Pier Pavilion) |

NOVEMBER

| 19 | LWF | Alexander | London (St James's Theatre) |

1905

MARCH

| 27 | AIH | Standing | Hastings (Pier Pavilion) |

MAY

| 7 | IoBE | Amateur | Berwick (Queen's Rooms) |

JUNE

8 LWF Amateur Chelmsford (Borough Theatre)

AUGUST

19 WoNI Morell & M London (Elephant and Castle Theatre)

SEPTEMBER

23 AIH Dansey London (Coronet Theatre)

OCTOBER

2 AIH Dansey London (Alexandra Theatre, Stoke
Newington)

16 AIH Dansey Southend (Empire Theatre) 3

22 AIH Dansey Newcastle (Theatre Royal) 1

30 AIH Dansey Cambridge (New Theatre) 2

NOVEMBER

6 AIH Dansey London (Grand Theatre, Fulham)

9 AIH Dansey Worcester (Theatre Royal) 3

20 AIH Dansey Glasgow (Royalty Theatre) 1

27 AIH Dansey Middlesborough (Theatre Royal) 2

1906

MAY

5 IoBE Amateur London (Public Hall, West Norwood)

NOVEMBER

14 LWF Amateur Birmingham (Grand Theatre) 1

1907

APRIL

23 IoBE Amateur Bath (Assembly Rooms) fit-up

13	IoBE	Hoffe	Croydon (Grand Theatre)
16	AIH	Amateur	London (Imperial Theatre)
20	IoBE	Hoffe	Bath (Theatre Royal) 2
22	WoNI	Tree	London (His Majesty's Theatre)
29	IoBE	Hoffe	Manchester (Theatre Royal) 1

JUNE

3	IoBE	Hoffe	Leeds (Grand Theatre) 1
3	AIH	Dansey	Sheffield (Lyceum Theatre) 1
13	IoBE	Hoffe	Whitby (The Spa Theatre)
17	IoBE	Hoffe	Hull (Theatre Royal) 1
24	IoBE	Hoffe	Glasgow (King's Theatre) 1

JULY

| 25 | IoBE | Hoffe | Southport (Opera House) 2 |
| 29 | IoBE | Hoffe | Swansea (Grand Theatre) |

AUGUST

5	AIH	Norris	Manchester (Theatre Royal) 1
8	LWF	Norris	Hull (Grand Theatre)
8	IoBE	Hoffe	Manchester (Queen's Theatre) 2
12	AIH	Norris	Hull (Grand Theatre)
12	LWF	Hoffe	Swansea (Grand Theatre)
22	LWF	Hoffe	Manchester (Queen's Theatre) 2

SEPTEMBER

2	IoBE	Hoffe	Dublin (Gaiety Theatre) 1
2	LWF	Hoffe	Dublin (Gaiety Theatre) 1
9	IoBE	Hoffe	Glasgow (Royalty Theatre) 1
9	LWF	Hoffe	Glasgow (Royalty Theatre) 1
23	LWF	Hoffe	York (Theatre Royal) 2
30	LWF	Hoffe	Lincoln (Theatre Royal) 3

| 28 | IoBE | Hoffe | Ipswich (Lyceum Theatre) 3 |
| 29 | LWF | Hoffe | Ipswich (Lyceum Theatre) 3 |

NOVEMBER

4	AIH	Norris	Brighton (West Pier)
7	LWF	Hoffe	Leamington (Theatre Royal)
7	IoBE	Hoffe	Leamington (Theatre Royal)
18	IoBE	Hoffe	Bradford (Theatre Royal) 1
18	LWF	Hoffe	Bradford (Theatre Royal) 1
25	IoBE	Hoffe	Worthing (Theatre Royal) 3
25	LWF	Hoffe	Worthing (Theatre Royal) 3

DECEMBER

2	LWF	Hoffe	Tunbridge Wells (Opera House)
2	IoBE	Hoffe	Tunbridge Wells (Opera House)
10	LWF	Hoffe	Sheffield (Lyceum Theatre) 1

1908

FEBRUARY

| 25 | IoBE | Hoffe | London (Scala Theatre) |

MARCH

| Nd | IoBE | Hoffe | Belfast (Opera House) |
| Nd | IoBE | Hoffe | Harrogate (Grand Opera House) |

APRIL

| 4 | IoBE | Amateur | Northampton (St. Andrew's Hospital) |
| 10 | IoBE | Amateur | Leeds (Leeds College of Music) |

JUNE

| 26 | IoBE | Hoffe | Leeds (Leeds College of Dramatic Art) |

Plays

LWF	Lady Windermere's Fan
WoNI	A Woman of No Importance
AIH	An Ideal Husband
IoBE	The Importance of Being Earnest

Companies

Waller & M	Lewis Waller and H H Morell
Morell & M	H H Morell and Frederick Mouillot
Alexander	George Alexander
Tapping	A B Tapping
Hawtrey	Charles Hawtrey
Varna	H W Varna
Myrlyn	Miss Paula Myrlyn
Bandman	Maurice E Bandman
Cressy	Miss Nina Cressy
Homer	Miss Beatrice Homer
Lanham	Miss Elsie Lanham/ Elsie Lanham and Alfred Selwyn
Waller	Lewis Waller
Thalberg	T B Thalberg/ T B Thalberg and Marion Terry
Klein	Cecil Klein and Fred Ash
Cooke	J Y F Cooke
Hare	Arthur Hare
Pardoe	Miss May Pardoe
Hartley	Charles Hartley
Anglesey	Marquis of Anglesey
Dansey	Herbert Dansey
Hoffe	Monckton Hoffe/ Hoffe and Campbell
Norris	Ernest E Norris

COMPANIES

The names of members of touring companies have, in the main, been drawn from newspaper reports, where spellings vary and many actors are not mentioned. There are therefore large gaps in the information for some companies.

LADY WINDERMERE'S FAN

Monckton Hoffe Company

Lord Windermere	Monckton Hoffe
Lady Windermere	Miss Nona Hoffe
Lord Darlington	H Lane Bayliff
Lord Augustus Lorton	Ralph Wollaston Hutton
Mr Dumby	
Duchess of Berwick	Miss Maud Henderson
Lady Agatha Carlisle	
Lady Jedburgh	
Mrs Erlynne	Miss Lydia Busch
Lady Stutfield	
Parker	
Rosalie	
Hopper	
Cecil Graham	Aubrey Fitzmaurice

The company also included: Miss Winifred Vallant.

Elsie Lanham and Alfred Selwyn Company

Lord Windermere	Alfred Selwyn
Lady Windermere	Edith G Ralph
	Armine Grace
	Yvonne Richardson (possibly Orchardson)
Lord Darlington	G E Clive
	Roy Cushing
	Leon Ainscliffe
Lord Augustus Lorton	Roy Cushing
	Malcolm Douglas
	Fred Ashe
Mr Dumby	Gerald Alexander
	James Quin
Duchess of Berwick	May Bowerman
	Maud Henderson
	Audrey Canning
Lady Agatha Carlisle	
Lady Jedburgh	Irene Clifton
	Ivy Stredwicke
Mrs Erlynne	Elsie Lanham
Lady Stutfield	
Parker	Mr Saxham
Rosalie	
Hopper	Fred J Haming
Cecil Graham	

The company also included: M Hylton Allen; Ruby StJohn Hall.

Charles Hartley Company

Lord Windermere
Lady Windermere   Miss R Mayne Young
Lord Darlington   F Dudman Bromwich
Lord Augustus Lorton   Frederick Loyd
Mr Dumby   Brember Wills
Duchess of Berwick   Miss Phillis Noell
Lady Agatha Carlisle
Lady Jedburgh
Mrs Erlynne   Ethel Gordon Paull
Lady Stutfield
Parker
Rosalie
Hopper
Cecil Graham

The company also included: Charles Hartley, Miss R Mayne Young, Miss Ethel Beale, Miss Di Forbes, Guy Carew, Arthur Ricketts.

Olga Brandon Company

Lord Windermere	Ernest Leicester
Lady Windermere	Emmie O'Reilly
Lord Darlington	Mr Austin-Leigh
Lord Augustus Lorton	George Hawtrey
Mr Dumby	Mr Finser-Taylor
Duchess of Berwick	
Lady Agatha Carlisle	
Lady Jedburgh	
Mrs Erlynne	Olga Brandon
Lady Stutfield	
Parker	
Rosalie	
Hopper	
Cecil Graham	Orlando Barnett

Nina Cressy Company

Lord Windermere	Doveton Maxwell
	J Cooke Beresford
Lady Windermere	Maud Evelyn
Lord Darlington	Percy D Standing
Lord Augustus Lorton	
Mr Dumby	
Duchess of Berwick	
Lady Agatha Carlisle	
Lady Jedburgh	
Mrs Erlynne	Nina Cressy
Lady Stutfield	
Parker	
Rosalie	
Hopper	Herbert Dunbar
Cecil Graham	

The company also included: Percy H Vernon, Arthur Mortimer, Hylton Allen, Gertrude Sterrell, Olive Loftus Leyton, Avril Leigh, Clarice Stuart, M Lyton.

Bandman and Wallace Company

Lord Windermere	Maurice Bandman
Lady Windermere	Lillie Thurlow
Lord Darlington	Drew Mackintosh
Lord Augustus Lorton	J W Hedges
Mr Dumby	
Duchess of Berwick	Mary Denver
Lady Agatha Carlisle	
Lady Jedburgh	
Mrs Erlynne	Gertrude Evans
Lady Stutfield	
Parker	
Rosalie	
Hopper	
Cecil Graham	

T B Thalberg Company

Lord Windermere	T B Thalberg
Lady Windermere	Eva Hamblin
	Gertrude Burnett
Lord Darlington	J Cooke Beresford
Lord Augustus Lorton	F Owen Baxter
Mr Dumby	Charles Esdaile
Duchess of Berwick	Elsie Carew
Lady Agatha Carlisle	Ella Dixon
Lady Jedburgh	Miss Grogan
Mrs Erlynne	Marion Terry
Lady Stutfield	Miss F Harrington
Parker	C Rivers Bertram
Rosalie	Miss F Cummings
Hopper	James Gelderd
Cecil Graham	Randolph E Reade

Paula Myrlyn Company

Lord Windermere	George H Harker
Lady Windermere	Maud Paget
Lord Darlington	William Sequin
Lord Augustus Lorton	Trent Adams
Mr Dumby	Douglas Miller
Duchess of Berwick	Mrs Gordon Gray
Lady Agatha Carlisle	Maud Evelyn
Lady Jedburgh	Amy Kirke
Mrs Erlynne	Paula Myrlyn
Lady Stutfield	
Parker	
Rosalie	Ella Rosa
Hopper	W G Buss
Cecil Graham	Arthur Godshall

A WOMAN OF NO IMPORTANCE

Beatrice Homer Company

Lord Illingworth	Leyton Cancellor
Mrs Arbuthnot	Beatrice Homer
Hester Worsley	Violet Greville
	Alys Eden
Mrs Allonby	Florence Henwood
	Constance Elgin
Lady Stutfield	Kathleen Russell
Lady Caroline Pontefract	Adeline Lester
	Bessie Armitage
Lady Hunstanton	Mrs J W Broughton
	Gertrude Le Sage
Gerald Arbuthnot	Gerald Mirrielees
	William Ashdowne
Sir John Pontefract	Basil Lascelles
	J E Savery
Lord Alfred Rufford	
Mr Kelvil	W J Butler
Daubeny	Herbert Greville

Charles Hartley Company

Lord Illingworth	
Mrs Arbuthnot	
Hester Worsley	
Mrs Allonby	Ethel Gordon Paull
Lady Stutfield	
Lady Caroline Pontefract	
Lady Hunstanton	
Gerald Arbuthnot	F Dudman Bromwich
Sir John Pontefract	
Lord Alfred Rufford	
Mr Kelvil	
Daubeny	

The company also included: Charles Hartley, Miss R Mayne Young, Miss Ethel Beale, Miss Di Forbes, Guy Carew, Arthur Ricketts.

Beerbohm Tree Company

Lord Illingworth	Beerbohm Tree
Mrs Arbuthnot	Marion Terry
Hester Worsley	Viola Tree
Mrs Allonby	Ellis Jeffreys
Lady Stutfield	Kate Cutler
Lady Caroline Pontefract	Kate Bishop
Lady Hunstanton	Mrs Charles Calvert
Gerald Arbuthnot	Charles Quartermaine
Sir John Pontefract	J Fisher White
Lord Alfred Rufford	Langhorne Burton
Mr Kelvil	Charles Allan
Daubeny	Edmund Maurice

J Y F Cooke Company

Lord Illingworth
Mrs Arbuthnot
Hester Worsley
Mrs Allonby
Lady Stutfield
Lady Caroline Pontefract
Lady Hunstanton
Gerald Arbuthnot
Sir John Pontefract
Lord Alfred Rufford
Mr Kelvil
Daubeny

Charles V France
Miss Madge McIntosh
Miss May Congdon
Miss Mary Raby
Violet Grace
Miss Mabel Derrie
Isabel Grey
A Hylton Allen

The company also included: Charles la Trobe, Richard Mason, J Y F Cooke, Stanley Dobie.

Lewis Waller Company

Lord Illingworth   Lewis Waller
Mrs Arbuthnot   Mrs Waller
Hester Worsley   Annie Webster
Mrs Allonby   Geraldine Oliffe
Lady Stutfield   Mrs Heslewood
Lady Caroline Pontefract   Amy Singleton
Lady Hunstanton   Mary Rorke
Gerald Arbuthnot   Herbert Beaumont
Sir John Pontefract   T Heslewood
Lord Alfred Rufford   Whitworth Jones
Mr Kelvil   Charles Goodhart
Daubeny   W Kitteridge (Kittredge)
Alice   Rachel Donne

Morrell and Mouillot Company

Lord Illingworth	H R Conway
	Frederick Mouillot
Mrs Arbuthnot	Miss Lingard
Hester Worsley	Rose Ralph
	Gertrude Davison
	Ruth Ellesmere
Mrs Allonby	Beatrice Homer
	Annie Stalman
Lady Stutfield	Muriel Johnson
	Christine Beauclerc
Lady Caroline Pontefract	Mrs Henry Kitts
Lady Hunstanton	Minnie Mouillot
	Miss Leslie Greenwood
Gerald Arbuthnot	J H Beaumont
Sir John Pontefract	Dallas Welford
	Mr Langdale
Lord Alfred Rufford	C R Simpson
Mr Kelvil	Leyton Cancellor
Daubeny	T N Walter

H W Varna Company

Lord Illingworth	H W Varna
Mrs Arbuthnot	Mrs Albert Barker
	Kay Glover
	Mrs Leslie James
Hester Worsley	Lily Roselle
	Alice Neilson
Mrs Allonby	Maud Rowlstone
	Margaret Murray
Lady Stutfield	Daisy Carton
	Marie Stuart
Lady Caroline Pontefract	Mrs Bradley
	Miss Carthew
Lady Hunstanton	Claire Pauncefort
	Miss Anson
	Mrs F Coplestone
Gerald Arbuthnot	E H Brooke
	Claude King
	Allan Mayhew
Sir John Pontefract	B Owen
Lord Alfred Rufford	H Molyneux Seel
Mr Kelvil	A P Kaye
Daubeny	Stanley Grahame

Kendal Chalmers Company

Lord Illingworth   Charles Hartley
Mrs Arbuthnot   Miss Lillian Williams
Hester Worsley
Mrs Allonby
Lady Stutfield
Lady Caroline Pontefract
Lady Hunstanton   Miss Mary Moody
Gerald Arbuthnot
Sir John Pontefract
Lord Alfred Rufford
Mr Kelvil
Daubeny

AN IDEAL HUSBAND

Waller and Morrell Company (original)

Robert Chiltern	Lewis Waller
Lady Chiltern	Julia Neilson
Mrs Cheveley	Florence West
Earl of Caversham	Alfred Bishop
Lord Goring	Charles Hawtrey
Viscomte de Nanjac	Cosmo Stuart
Mr Montford	Henry Stanford
Lady Markby	Fanny Brough
	Vane Featherstone
Countess of Basildon	Vane Featherstone
	Enid Spencer Brunton
Mrs Marchmont	Helen Forsyth
Mabel Chiltern	Maud Millet
Mason	H Deane
Phipps	Charles Brookfield

Sarah Thorne Company

Robert Chiltern	Frank Gillmore
Lady Chiltern	Stella Hazlewood
Mrs Cheveley	Anne Beaufort
Earl of Caversham	Denis Coyne
Lord Goring	Cosmo Stuart
Viscomte de Nanjac	Charles Troode
Mr Montford	
Lady Markby	Emily Thorne
Countess of Basildon	Miss Dagmar
Mrs Marchmont	Miss Herbert
Mabel Chiltern	Miss Douglas
Mason	Mr Payne
Phipps	W H Powell

Waller and Morrell (touring)

Robert Chiltern
Lady Chiltern
Mrs Cheveley   Vane Featherstone
Earl of Caversham
Lord Goring   Fred Terry
Viscomte de Nanjac
Mr Montford
Lady Markby
Countess of Basildon
Mrs Marchmont
Mabel Chiltern
Mason
Phipps

Charles Hawtrey Company

Robert Chiltern	Frank Fenton
	Rudge Harding
Lady Chiltern	Gwynne Herbert
Mrs Cheveley	Alma Stanley
Earl of Caversham	Fred Emery
Lord Goring	Cosmo Stuart
	"Cossie" Gordon Lennox
Viscomte de Nanjac	R Temple
Mr Montford	
Lady Markby	Mrs Arthur Hayes
Countess of Basildon	Constance Collier
Mrs Marchmont	Adie Burt
Mabel Chiltern	Adie Burt
	Audrey Ford
Mason	
Phipps	H J Ford

Nina Cressy Company

Robert Chiltern	D Maxwell
	Cyril Harrison
Lady Chiltern	Octavia Kenmore
	Beatrice Constance
Mrs Cheveley	Nina Cressy
Earl of Caversham	Percy H Vernon
Lord Goring	Percy D Standing
Viscomte de Nanjac	Arthur Mortimer
Mr Montford	
Lady Markby	
Countess of Basildon	
Mrs Marchmont	
Mabel Chiltern	Maud Evelyn
Mason	
Phipps	

Marquis of Anglesey Company

Robert Chiltern	Ernest Vere
Lady Chiltern	Florence Tyrell
Mrs Cheveley	Florence Hamer
Earl of Caversham	Gerald Alexander
Lord Goring	Marquis of Anglesey
	Cecil Newton
Viscomte de Nanjac	Cecil Newton
Mr Montford	Arthur Hickman
Lady Markby	Agnes [or Doris?] Thomas
Countess of Basildon	Dora Vayne
Mrs Marchmont	Madge Campbell
Mabel Chiltern	Florence Tempest
Mason	James Halford
Phipps	Douglas Hamilton

The company also included: Ferdinand Conti.

Edward O'Neill and Herbert Dansey Company

Robert Chiltern	Edward O'Neill
Lady Chiltern	Charlotte Granville
Mrs Cheveley	Elizabeth Meller
Earl of Caversham	George Bealby
Lord Goring	Austin Melroy
	Herbert Dansey
Viscomte de Nanjac	Eric Maxon
Mr Montford	Claude Harris
Lady Markby	Isabel Grey
Countess of Basildon	Miss R Mayne Young
Mrs Marchmont	Gertrude Millar
Mabel Chiltern	Kittie Grattan
Mason	Frank Earle
Phipps	Lionel Glenister

The company also included: H. Athol Ford, R. Redman, Eugene Verney, Jeannette Legros, Gertrude Faucett, Mona Travers.

Ernest E Norris Company

Robert Chiltern
Lady Chiltern
Mrs Cheveley
Earl of Caversham
Lord Goring
Viscomte de Nanjac
Mr Montford
Lady Markby
Countess of Basildon
Mrs Marchmont
Mabel Chiltern
Mason
Phipps

The company included: Ernest E Norris, Vera Beringer, Henry Renouf, E Petley, Miss Helena Parsons, Miss Enid Ross, Miss Bessie Harrison.

THE IMPORTANCE OF BEING EARNEST

George Alexander Company (original)

John Worthing	George Alexander
Algernon Moncrieffe	Allan Aynesworth
Gwendolen	Irene Vanburgh
Cicely	Evelyn Millard
	Violet Lyster
Lady Bracknell	Rose Leclerq
	Mrs Edward Saker
Miss Prism	Mrs George Canninge
Canon Chasuble	H H Vincent
Lane	F Kinsey Peile
Merriman	Frank Dyall

Elsie Lanham Company

John Worthing	Alfred Selwyn
Algernon Moncrieffe	Roy Cushing
Gwendolen	Elsie Lanham
Cicely	Yvonne Richardson
Lady Bracknell	Maud Henderson
Miss Prism	
Canon Chasuble	
Lane	
Merriman	

Monckton Hoffe Company

John Worthing	C Nicholson
	H Layne-Bayliff
Algernon Moncrieffe	Monckton Hoffe
Gwendolen	Minnie (or Winnie) Grey
	Lydia Busch
Cicely	Miss Hester Newton
	Nona Hoffe
Lady Bracknell	Kate Osborne
	Ada Melrose
	Phyllis Manners
Miss Prism	Amy Lloyd-Desmond
Canon Chasuble	Ralph Hutton
Lane	A W Barker
Merriman	Arthur Forbes [Waite?]
	Aubrey Fitzmaurice

Arthur Hare Company

John Worthing
Algernon Moncrieffe
Gwendolen
Cicely
Lady Bracknell
Miss Prism
Canon Chasuble
Lane
Merriman

The company included: Arthur Hare, Caleb Porter, Cyril Scott, A E Goddard, G B Baker, Iden Payne, E Musprat, Miss Florence Tyrrell, Miss E Marsden.

Frank Weathersby Company

John Worthing	Harold Weston
Algernon Moncrieffe	Julian D'Albie
Gwendolen	May Saker
Cicely	Margaret Boyd
Lady Bracknell	Maud Kirwan
Miss Prism	Dot Seilby
Canon Chasuble	Edwin Mervyn
Lane	Harold Bariston
Merriman	Eric H Albury

George Alexander Company (touring)

John Worthing	George Alexander
Algernon Moncrieffe	W Graham Browne
Gwendolen	Mabel Dubois (tour)
	Margaret Halstan (St James revival)
Cicely	Lilian Braithwaite
Lady Bracknell	Miss M Talbot
Miss Prism	Mrs Thomas Laverton (tour)
	Bessie Page (St James revival)
Canon Chasuble	E Lyall Swete
Lane	Lennox Pawle (tour)
	Herbert Dansey (St James revival)
Merriman	R E Goddard

A B Tapping Company

John Worthing	A B Tapping
Algernon Moncrieffe	Julius Knight
	Roland Mure
Gwendolen	Henrietta Watson
	Alice Dukes
Cicely	Alice Farleigh
Lady Bracknell	Ida Molesworth
	Mrs Albert Barker
Miss Prism	Helen Rous
	Minnie Mouillot
Canon Chasuble	W R Staveley
	J W Miller
Lane	Hugh Goring
	Mr Douglas
Merriman	D Mackintosh

May Pardoe Company

John Worthing
Algernon Moncrieffe
Gwendolen
Cicely
Lady Bracknell   Miss May Pardoe
Miss Prism
Canon Chasuble
Lane
Merriman

The company also included: Courtenay Thorpe, Walter Ringham, Edward Bonfield, John Ford, Richard Kenyon, Miss Marion Grey, Miss Olive Wilton, Miss Lola Duncan.

John Worthing	Wilfred Foster
Algernon Moncrieffe	Orlando Barnett
Gwendolen	Miss K Harwood
Cicely	Violet Lister
Lady Bracknell	M'Aimee Murray
Miss Prism	Minna Blakiston
Canon Chasuble	W R Staveley
Lane	W Smithson
Merriman	J Graves